In *Done Right*, celebrated chef Teo Paul invites readers into the kitchens that made him: from Paris and Piedmont to Toronto's Ossington strip and the wild beauty of Grey County. With over 70 comforting, soul-satisfying recipes from his four acclaimed restaurants—Union, Côte de Bœuf, Heart's Tavern, and Le Tambour—and his formative years cooking in the kitchens of Europe, Teo shares the flavors and stories behind a career that helped define Toronto's food scene.

Whether you're a home cook chasing flavor or a restaurant lover reliving your favorite meal, Teo shows readers how to cook with both hands, a full heart, and deep intention. Within the pages of *Done Right*, you'll find:

- **UNION FAVORITES**: Union Salad, Steak Tartare, Sticky Ribs, Polenta Gratin, and Sticky Ginger Cake
- **FRENCH BISTRO CLASSICS**: French Onion Soup, Côte de Bœuf with Peppercorn Sauce, Mousse au Chocolat, and Paris Bistro Tarte Tatin
- **ITALIAN INSPIRATIONS**: Gnocchi Bolognese, Bagna Cauda Beefsteak Tomato Salad, and Italian Ferry Arancini
- **RUSTIC CANADIAN COMFORTS**: Halibut with Shrimp Butter Sauce, Tamworth Pork Chop, Heart's Smash Burger, and Maple Croissant Bread Pudding

Done Right traces Teo's restaurant journey—with moments of risk, resilience, and revelation, each captured in a recipe made with boldness and heart. Through evocative storytelling, personal essays, and the photography of Daniel Neuhaus, this intimate cookbook captures the glow of candlelit bistros, the hum of service, and the simple truth that great cooking isn't about perfection—it's about presence.

Done Right

HEARTFELT RECIPES FROM A LIFE IN RESTAURANTS

Teo Paul

appetite
by RANDOM HOUSE

Library and Archives Canada Cataloguing in Publication is available upon request.
ISBN: 978-0-525-61305-3
eBook ISBN: 978-0-525-61306-0

Some of the recipes in this book may include raw eggs, meat, or fish. When these foods are consumed raw, there is always the risk that bacteria may be present. For recipes calling for the raw foods, always buy certified salmonella-free eggs and the freshest meat and fish available from a reliable grocer, storing them in the refrigerator until they are served. Because of the health risks associated with the consumption of bacteria that can be present in raw eggs, meat, and fish, these foods should not be consumed by infants, small children, pregnant women, the elderly, or any persons who may be immunocompromised.

Book and cover design by Jennifer Griffiths
Photography by Daniel Neuhaus
Photograph on page 25 (top right corner) by Barbara Allain
Typeset by Erin Cooper

Printed in China

The authorized representative in the EU for product safety and compliance is Penguin Random House Ireland, Morrison Chambers, 32 Nassau Street, Dublin D02 YH68, Ireland, https://eu-contact.penguin.ie

Published in Canada by Appetite by Random House®,
a division of Penguin Random House Canada Limited.
320 Front Street West, Suite 1400
Toronto, Ontario, M5V 3B6, Canada
penguinrandomhouse.ca

10 9 8 7 6 5 4 3 2 1

appetite by RANDOM HOUSE | Penguin Random House Canada

This book is dedicated to my dad, Michael, who believed in me, backed me, gave Union its name, and helped me build it with his love and his eye for all those little and big things you see in there. And to my daughter, June, whose awesome spirit gave me the courage and will to keep going when everything felt lost and broken.

Contents

Paris and Piedmont

Union

Côte de Bœuf

Heart's

Le Tambour

Pantry

Introduction

BEGINNING

My grandmother liked to make roasted potatoes to ground herself when she got home from long trips. She'd tell me this as I helped her finish cooking dinner. I was 10 years old and she, in her mid-60s. She had this perfect heavy-bottomed aluminum pan, and they'd go in peeled and cut in half, flat face down so they'd have a crispy side and be fluffy inside. When they came out of the oven, she'd scrape them off the pan to reveal their golden crisp underbelly. Sometimes she'd use bacon fat to roast them. As we put the finishing touches on dinner, she'd share the way she did things, while my grandfather would be in the backyard with a pork roast turning on the barbecue. If he didn't have a roast, he'd be grilling a top sirloin from the A&P grocery in Stouffville, Ontario.

We'd go visit them on Sundays around five p.m., walking up to their white brick bungalow with its dark green shingled roof, up the gray stone slab steps to the front door, which had Swiss cowbells hanging on the back that would clatter and bang when you turned the etched silver knob and pushed your way in. And immediately you'd be hit with the wonderful, warm, sweet, musky, savory smell of love and cooking that the home had been conjuring since the 1950s. On the left was a little breakfast nook with a pine table holding a toaster oven and a lamp and salt and pepper shakers. To the right was the galley kitchen, with an olive-colored fridge, a faux wood counter, and an electric stove on one side, and the sink and a long counter on the other, with a phone hanging on the wall.

You could glance around and see what was for dinner. An apple pie would be sitting by the phone, and there'd be a top sirloin steak on a platter next to it, with a ton of ground black pepper, a pinch of garlic and onion powder, and a splash of soy and Worcestershire sauce. It would have been handled, rubbed, and flipped by my grandfather, who had pale blue eyes and was the town doctor. By the time I came around, he had already delivered over 2,000 babies. He'd often get paid with chickens and pork, until my grandmother took over his billing. We called him Johnny, but he was known in town as Dr. Button. His father, Ernie, ran the town hardware store, selling Model T Fords and marriage licenses and bathtubs. My grandfather lived his whole life on the same street. He was born in a house at the top and built a house at the end, by a farm with a light blue barn and a cornfield. When my grandparents heard the door open, they'd come to greet you, beaming and smiling, with raised-pitch, excited, welcoming voices.

With the steak, there'd be my grandmother's chili sauce, made with plum tomatoes and green peppers and peaches, and there'd be mustard and horseradish in little white wing-tipped bowls on the dark oak dining table. If the meal was rotisserie pork, she'd go to the pantry in the basement and pull out her chunk pickle relish, then go to the fridge to grab the Nance's Mustard they would bring back from Florida. Broccoli with cheese sauce was a frequent side. I'd watch her make the roux and pour in the milk, whisking it slowly in her 1950s aluminum cookware—her strong, curled, arthritic hands bent at the fingertips from gardening and peeling and worrying. She'd get me to grate the sharp Cheddar she'd have tucked in the door of the fridge. This was dinner at their place.

In the summer, there would always be strawberries next to the sink, waiting to be stemmed and cut and made into jam, Roma tomatoes for chutney, pickling cucumbers, and baby corn she'd pick from the cornfield that surrounded their backyard. At five o'clock, you could hear the distant whistle of the last train leaving for the city cascading across the fields. Her apple pie had a simple flaky pastry she made with lard, and just sugar and a squeeze of lemon on the apples. She'd serve it with a sharp Cheddar cheese. Some nights she'd flambé bananas, finishing them with a brandy that would light up on the pan, and serve them with ice cream.

If we slept over, my grandfather would cook us eggs and bacon in the morning. His sweet spot was scrambled eggs, because that was how he liked them, but you could get poached or fried, and sometimes over easy if he was up for it. But scrambled eggs were his specialty. He'd put them in sunny-side up in sizzling butter and wait until they were half cooked, then scramble them in the pan at the last moment with a good dose of black pepper and salt. The bundle of eggs would hit the plate white and yellow with specks of black pepper. We'd have bacon and toast and my grandmother's frozen strawberry jam. For lunch there'd be sandwiches cut in fours, made with cold sliced pork or steak, butter, and mustard on fresh Italian bread from the bakery around the corner, with her bread-and-butter pickles on the side. They ate like this whether we were there or not.

❖

I grew up in Toronto, on Tranby Avenue. There was a main street at the end of it, with a strip of good little restaurants. In the fall, when the nights were misty and full of leaves, I can remember the smells of food from the hood exhausts of those restaurants. There was a French-Lebanese restaurant called Arlequin, a few Italian spots, and a steak frites place called L'Entrecôte. As a kid, I felt an intimacy with their kitchens, churning out dinners for the city. I'd imagine the joy and laughter of the dining rooms and the chatter from the little bars tucked on the side. We ate out a lot as a family, and Arlequin was where we went the most. Inside, we nestled in the booth as a family. It was where my father seemed happiest and most engaged, and we all brought our best selves. At home, he'd retreat to his room, and we'd find our own spots as well.

So the restaurants around our house, and the smells coming out of them in the autumn air, both calmed me and exhilarated me at the same time.

My father left when I was 11. I was a shy kid in the middle of my younger brother, Chasen, who was 6 at the time, and my older sister, Amy, who was 14. Being in the middle, I soaked up my mother's pain, and her utterances over my dad's absence. I felt responsible for looking after her, and the heaviness that came with that marked the end of my childhood. I'd meet my dad for lunch in a restaurant once a week, and although it felt strange, those restaurants became my refuge, where I could suspend reality and still feel like my father was a part of the family.

I got my first kitchen job when I was 16, at Arlequin—that French bistro around the corner. They had a lunch takeout counter at the front. I worked there, serving cold salads of curried chicken with apples and ratatouille and hummus and baba ghanoush. Six months in, the older well-dressed ladies amused themselves by shaming me with the line "Oh, don't worry, we know it's your first day" as I continued to stumble about, awkwardly digging into the platter of hummus to get a good scoop into the takeout container and fumbling with the grilled vegetables before poking and mumbling about the cash register to cash them out. But every once in a while, the owner and chef would let me in the kitchen, hand me a bucket of apricots for jam, and send me to cut and pit in the driveway by the garbage. Later on, he'd come out and scream at me for being back there—until he realized he'd asked me to be. It wasn't much to begin with, but I got to go behind the curtain and walk through the bustling clash and bang of the kitchen. The fiery-hot line was the first thing you saw, with its big grill and the rolling ceiling heat of the salamander, the lit stoves with sizzling pans, the plates clattering up with steak frites and rabbit Dijonnaise, and the smells wafting out.

For a moment, I was part of the frenzy of movement and dance, and I felt a reverence and excitement for what they did. I grew fond of the chef, Chris Mathias, and came to call him a friend. Just having the chance to walk through the kitchen and grab the apricots from the fridge was enough for me to tell myself I'd made it further than I could have imagined. It was only a beginning, but it lit the path that would shape the rest of my life in kitchens. What follows is where that path has led, and the dishes that defined it.

THIS BOOK

This book traces my own journey, which led me to Paris as a young man, then to Piedmont, then home again to open my first restaurant, Union, with my father. And everything after that.

These are cooking moments from my life, shared to inspire any cook—at any level—to lean into the dish you're making, fully engaged and present. Cook with both hands, embracing a process that invites intention and heart, because the people you're feeding can feel that. It's what makes great food come alive. To be clear, this is the opposite of cooking hunched over a recipe, assembling the dish without that intention. That kind of dish falls flat. This cookbook is meant to have force—I've filled it with presence, boldness, and love. Any cook drawn to a recipe already has a sense of what that dish should be. That little nudge—that pull—is the moment I'm talking about. No one can cook it better than the one who feels it most.

These recipes come from that place. They are a collection of dig-deep moments. When I needed to cook something *great*, like on Union's opening night, for my first apartment dinner in Paris, or when cooking at Nico's hotel. Times when I needed a wow to save my ass because I had put myself far enough out there to either sink or swim. And what followed was a kind of magic—a jolt of love that cuts through doubt and hits the core of what matters most. That's the spot to find when you cook.

For me, it started at my grandparents' house when I was a kid. The nurturing love. The everyday cooking moves they mastered over a lifetime, like my grandmother's pies and crumbles, and my grandfather's marinades for steaks and roasts he'd grilled on the barbecue under a big crabapple tree. That was my buoy, my foundation. But I had to put myself far enough out there to find and recognize it.

The dishes I'm offering are my hits—what surfaced from writing the book, and what sparked four successful restaurants. They're fastballs down the middle, intended for the cook to hit farther than I ever could. All they ask of the one making them is to be fiercely engaged. To swing hard. Because when you connect and it's done right, the food becomes bold and vibrant, heartfelt and alive.

TABAC
RUE
DE BRETAGNE
l'Atelier
1er ETAGE
TABAC
TABAC
CHUT!

Paris and Piedmont

AU PETIT FER A CHEVAL
CAFÉ ET LAIT
BIÈRE
Brune & Blonde
APÉRITIFS DE MARQUES
TÉLÉPHONE
Paris-Province
Archives 38-50
CAFÉ ET LAIT
LAIT CHAUD
CHOCOLAT ET THE
CONSOMMATIONS DE CHOIX
BIERE
BRUNE & BLONDE
TELEPHONE
GAZ

Paris

PART 1

I arrived in Paris in 2001, right before the euro came into currency. Armored trucks blazed down boulevards with sirens blaring as French old ladies clutched their purses and worried about the price of baguettes. The restaurant, SoMo, was not complete yet, so for the first 8 months I was helping with *bricolage*. Translation: construction. I was doing stuff I was terrible at, and all the while trying to understand the British humor of my bosses. The owners were expats with three successful Parisian bars, and this was their first big restaurant endeavor. They'd gutted the place, and it was freezing inside. I had brought my friend Chris Mathias (from the Arlequin days) over with me, thinking we'd cook together and grow our friendship, but he was 10 years older than me, a more established cook, and also English, so he fit right in with the new crew. Everyone asked him why I got the job as head chef and not him. I spent most of my time tucked away, stripping paint, feeling vulnerable, useless, and unwanted. I was very green and naive—my confidence was constantly wavering.

The place was on rue Montmartre, just off the Grands Boulevards in the 2nd arrondissement. It was south of Montmartre, where Sacre Coeur sits on a hilltop, so they named it SoMo. It was doomed from the start. It was a huge space with a second-floor mezzanine that wrapped around the whole place. The previous owner was a highly revered eccentric Frenchman adored by the neighborhood, and he had an eclectic wine list and cellar in the basement. We were not French, and they gutted the cellar and whatever magic was left in the space—there was no bridge to remedy that. To make it worse, after stripping the place down, they built it back up with black tile, stone, and metal, and the result was dark and moody and cold.

The kitchen, the one space they didn't bother to renovate, was in the basement next to the washrooms. But I liked that because it was built and designed by a Frenchman—an authentic Paris kitchen, broken down and hot as hell, and it stunk like a bygone kitchen that you'd pick through in an auction. There was a six-burner stove, a planche, two ovens, a fryer, and a walk-in at the far end. Lowboys and steel counters lined one wall, the dish pit the other, with a dumbwaiter carrying plates up and dirty dishes down. The room was lit by humming fluorescent tubes, walls patched with old drill holes, and a mustard-colored rubber floor worn thin by years of service. At the far end, a small workstation opened toward the beer fridge and the stone caverns beneath the street. This was to be my stage, where I would learn if I had "it" or not. A neglected, hot, broken, over-lit trench in the bowels of Paris—it was just as George Orwell described in *Down and Out in Paris and London*, and I could see him there, in the dank dish room in the depths of a fancy Paris hotel, amongst the catacombs. In my mind, he has his back to me and a sink with a tilted tower of dirty dishes in front of him.

By the time the place was ready, the owners had spent twice what they'd planned and pulled in 20 new investors, each tossing in a few thousand euros and acting like they owned the place. The air was tense; everyone wanted money back fast. Chris and I were barely speaking. It was hard not to feel that he had the stronger claim to the job. He'd put in his time. I hadn't. It was a lot to overcome, and I had a lot to lose.

Minutes before opening night, my father called. I thought he was phoning to wish me luck, but he didn't even know it was the night. He told me my mother had landed a job in Neuchâtel, Switzerland—then added that he wasn't going with her. It shouldn't have surprised me.

He'd left before, when I was 11, and came back a year and a half later. Still, it rattled me. As he talked, I drifted back to being a kid, hearing that same bright tone that said everything was fine, while my gut told me otherwise.

I was rattled, trying to process what I'd just heard, and when I went to open a Perrier bottle with my knife, as I'd seen Chris do smoothly and coolly many times, I stabbed myself in the bicep. I staggered around as a trickle of blood flowed down my arm. When I saw the white of my muscle, I sat on the counter, about to faint. Gio, one of the Croatian builders, was still there and made me eat a packet of sugar to keep me from going down. At the clinic, the doctor figured I'd been in a knife fight, so he grabbed my arm and gruffly stitched me up without any freezing, to teach me a lesson. My French was so bad that I could not tell him any different.

And that was how it all began.

Six months later, Chris left the restaurant and went out on his own. He had an English passport and could work anywhere. I was sponsored, so this was my only chance to stay in Paris. Things between us had turned bad. He'd been my cooking mentor and a friend, and it stung that he was well liked and I was not. From the moment we arrived, we'd been pegged against each other. One night, when I burned the bones for stock, he tore into me. He had never done that before, and I felt unworthy and embarrassed—an imposter in the trade. I hadn't gone to cooking school, didn't have knife skills, and couldn't clean a fish to save my life.

After he left, everything felt empty. The home my parents had made was gone, and I couldn't speak French. I was drinking all the time in little cafés, tabacs, and bars across the city. I was full of self-pity and ego, terrified to be on my own. My friend was gone, and so was my footing. I was taking hits in all my softest spots and didn't have the emotional literacy to understand what I was feeling.

Despite all this, I still loved to cook. I loved the trade, the hustle on the line, that dance you do to bang it out and chew through the chits

CAFE
AUX DEUX AMIS
COMPTOIR

that come tumbling in. And despite the occasional burnt bones, I was good at it. I just needed more time around the track, cooking and honing my skills. I missed Chris when he left, but was also freed from the constant comparison. I hoped now for a few good services to get my confidence back.

The restaurant was a short walk from the Bourse (the Paris stock exchange), so we had massive lunch services—100-plus covers a day. And the French appetite and budget for lunch were vast: entrée, plat, dessert. Steak, duck confit, swordfish, foie gras, sashimi—whatever you put on the plat du jour was devoured. It helped that I was in the basement, cut off from the people eating, unintimidated and unaffected by the riches of Paris. In my mind, I could have been cooking anywhere.

PART 2

Most days, the kitchen was a sweltering 90 degrees, and even hotter in the summer. But I started to find my rhythm down there. I developed a kind of intimacy with the dishes; as I cooked them over and over again, I instinctively knew how to finish them so that it felt as if the food was dancing onto the plate. And I was learning how to move in a kitchen with grace: how to duck, and weave, and hold, and press, and run, and shift around, and spin along the line. I started really nailing it and began having clean services no matter what was happening. I could rescue and coax whoever needed it at that moment, be it the salad guy in the weeds or a waiter who forgot an order. I could adjust on the fly and took pride in dragging us all to the finish line, one clean, perfect service after another.

I was cooking steak frites and poulet rôti, warm chèvre salad, duck confit with pommes sautées, and the occasional tagine or cassoulet. It was good food, but it wasn't authentically mine. I cooked what I was taught, and anytime I would try something new, I hit a wall of self-doubt and felt the imposter syndrome creep in. So I kept hammering out the hits. I wasn't cooking my own food yet, but I was learning lessons about simplicity and the vitalness of quality ingredients. Cooking in Paris, you have amazing products at your fingertips—it's both intimidating and awesome. The walk-in was full of chanterelles and girolles, and their pungent muskiness would permeate the room. Sweet French torpedo-shaped strawberries, white asparagus, foie gras, artisan ducks, still with their heads and feathers on, nestled in boxes when they arrived. Bright yellow des Landes chickens and silky white Bresse birds with feathers on their necks, blue feet, and the Label Rouge medallions on their breasts. One day, a striploin on the bone arrived, and you didn't have to know anything about beef to know it was special. It had a dark maroon hue with white-yellow fat marbled within and a thick, slightly yellowish fat cap. I could sense the lush wet grass the cow had grazed on, and the care of the feed it was finished on. I still remember it, angled on the counter, smelling aged and earthy and clean and wonderful. After that experience, I wanted every piece of meat to look and smell and feel just like that.

I cooked for another 3 years down there, but I was slowly turning into a troll in the heat and basement air. The whole thing was becoming a grind that I feared I would never escape. I wanted to be part of the busy clatter and clink and hustle of people above. The neighborhood was great for lunches, but the nights were hit-and-miss. Broken fridges and constant judgment, coupled with little encouragement or voice of my own. Rage and frustration were beginning to seep out of me. I was shot, frustrated, broken, hungover, and dehydrated most of the time. I felt a daily sting of helplessness and insignificance. I was full of resentment for Chris for leaving me in a pit I felt I could never dig myself out of. I was entrenched in hopelessness and failure and confusion and fear and the unfairness that no one ever recognized the work I was doing.

My right-hand man was Caesar, a soft-spoken Venezuelan who was married to a French woman. On one of my last days there, he said, "Teo, what are they going to do? Nobody can cook like you." It was finally the recognition I'd never gotten of how I could cook in the moment and create food that was dancing and vibrant. How it came off the stove—bold and glistening and purposeful—despite my torment and doubt amongst the clatter and chaos and neon lights and heat and fridge compressors wailing. It was subtle, and it was hard to explain, but he caught it. I'll always remember that, because I actually believed what he said. It wasn't because I was a great chef; I had crap knife skills and no school credentials. I had not come up with anything authentic and true. But that's not what he meant. He was talking about the way I cooked, how I stayed in the moment, so that when the food came to you, it felt loving and alive, as if it were your grandmother who was cooking down there. And there was magic in that, and even the imposter in me knew it. So I took it and set out to muster what I believed was missing in my cooking. I wanted to get out of the trench and see the people I was cooking for, so I started to cook for them in their apartments on the Left Bank.

PART 3

It all started when I rented an apartment off rue Montorgueil in the 2nd arrondissement, just around the corner from the restaurant. The entrance off the street had a set of large blue-gray doors that opened up to a cobblestone courtyard with beautiful trees and shrubs and the vast Paris sky above. My apartment was on the right side, on the second floor, with windows going all the way across. When you walked in, the bedroom was on the left, and then a hallway with a bathroom off it, and then it opened up into a large rectangular space. In the corner at the back, there was a square fireplace cut into the brick, and on the other side, a small open kitchen with four electric burners, an oval sink, and a counter with bar stools. It had rickety, wobbly, hardwood floors that would creak and squeal when you stepped on them.

It was a really fantastic place, but expensive too. I figured I could cook dinners there and turn the apartment into my restaurant to pay the rent. I asked a welder friend, Chad, from Kansas to cut me a mesh grill to fit the fireplace so I could do some cooking over the fire. I overheard that one of the regulars at the restaurant was turning 40, so I invited him to my place for dinner and told him to bring his friends and some wine to celebrate, and I'd cook a six-course meal. Just like Michael Stadtlander did. I had just moved in a few days earlier. I borrowed plates and cutlery and wine and water glasses and carafes for wine. I found a beat-up, long wood table, and I grabbed some chairs from the restaurant.

I got fresh croissants and tore them apart and soaked them overnight with egg yolks, sugar, and cream for a bread pudding with apples and a crème anglaise. I bought plump French quails, marinated them in red wine, and grilled them on the fire. I made olive bread and grilled it too. At the fishmonger's, I bought fresh scallops—still alive in their sandy shells. He showed me how to wedge a knife in and slit the tendon to spring them open. I cleaned them in the little sink, the smell of fresh sea water hitting me as the shells sprang open and juices ran down my hand. I cooked the scallops, liver and all, in butter, and poured the browned butter and lemon juice over them. I roasted a filet de bœuf on the fire and served it with seared foie gras, potato purée, and baby bok choy.

The crowd was boisterous and noisy. There were 14 of them, but it felt like 30. The fireplace had no draw, so the windows were wide open. By the end of the dinner there were ballads, serenades, stomping, marching, laughter, and applause, and the room was drenched in alcohol and thick with smoke. They stayed till two-thirty in the morning. The next day I had complaint letters stuffed under my door and pinned to the front of it. I did the dishes in the bathtub, mulling over the evening. It had been a success, but at what cost? I knew it wasn't sustainable. Still, Pierre, one of the guests, booked me soon after to cook at his brother-in-law's birthday.

I followed what I remembered from Stadtlander's farm, building my own routes through Paris to find the best products. I carried a big knapsack when I shopped. At the butcher in the 22nd arrondissement I waited with the old French ladies for sweetbreads and filet de bœuf.

J'aime Paris
Une Exposition de Photographies de
Peter Turnley
PRIX SERVICE COMPRIS

He showed me how to trim the membrane and spoon the butter over as they cooked. Those small exchanges became my schooling.

Around the corner was a small specialty shop for classic French ingredients—Magret duck, foie gras, tins of duck fat. Then the Japanese market for bonito, tempura mix, and sauces to accent the dinner. I'd finish at the grocery store for cream and eggs, and at the poissonnière for fish—often carrelet, a flat flounder-like fish with orange-red spots on its skin. Sweet and beautiful. I'd put it all in the fridge and make a dessert that was easy to carry—bread pudding or chocolate cake.

I hired a waitress named Anna, a Swedish woman with a Black Sabbath thing who called me Teo Boy. Before the events, I packed my knapsack and met her on the Métro by four-thirty. We had to be ready by seven. In the bag were my knives, tongs, whisk, cutting board, and a cast-iron pan. Fear always hit when I unpacked, hoping I hadn't forgotten anything. To calm myself, I thought of a time with my father when I was 16 and we were grilling 30 quails for a party. Flames hissed and spat every time the quails hit the grill. He stood behind me, stressed.

"Oh man, are we going to pull this off?" he said.

"Yes, we are."

"But how do you know?"

"I know because we fucking have to."

That was the "we fucking have to" moment—when everything is on fire and you have no choice but to keep going. That night the quails came out glazy and red and charred because they fucking had to be. I clung to that memory as I started to cook. I was always a little behind, and was working on two beers and an empty stomach most of the time. I felt a kinship with the amateur keyboardist thrown into Bob Dylan's "Like a Rolling Stone," struggling to keep up with the ever-increasing tempo. That authentic "oh shit" chase to keep up gave that song a force and spirit, and I felt it did the same for my dinners. So I kept trying to get comfortable in that "oh shit" moment and see what could happen from there.

That first night at Pierre's brother-in-law's place, I cooked my heart out. The stage was a light gray stone apartment with iron balconies—the classic Parisian Left Bank home you see in 90s movies. After dessert was served, I left the kitchen exhausted and relieved to be done. I was kicking myself over a few things, but I knew I had gotten enough right to make it special. I took in all the little details: the warm light of the dining room, how it played off the oak and mahogany furniture and the elegant couches and cloth curtains on the windows. As I approached the table of guests, everyone got up and started clapping and hollering. It was a rush.

We cleaned up quickly, stumbled out onto the small, busy street below, and caught a taxi to the Marais to catch last call. We went straight to Au Petit Fer à Cheval, my favorite spot in Paris, and squeezed our way into the crowd of people and leaned against the bar and celebrated. My friend Chris was there, and despite our falling-out, he grabbed me and said, "You're fucking doing it, Chef! You're really fucking doing it!"

More dinners came, but slowly and far apart. I started working at Rungis, the main food market for Paris—the largest wholesale market in the world—helping Chris buy for a company called Artisan Foods, run by an Irish woman, Natasha, and her brother Simon. They sold French vegetables, mushrooms, ducks, chickens, and foie gras to high-end restaurants in Dublin. My relationship with Chris had mended a little after I left SoMo; he got me the job. We'd meet at four in the morning, catch the bus to Rungis, and walk through the brightly lit airplane hangars full of chanterelles, girolles, cèpes, black truffles, red torpedo strawberries, and perfectly packed white asparagus, checking off the list. After selecting the best of everything, we'd send it to the dock, wrap and stack the pallets, and have them on their way to Dublin by noon.

When we were done, we'd head to our favorite part of the market—the meat hall. It was a massive cool room where wild boars, bright red blood on their hair, hung in rows. Bins of cow heads piled like masks. Beautiful marbled beef, Bresse chickens with blue feet, ducks laid gently in crates, rabbits tucked in wooden boxes as if asleep. In the middle of it all was a glassed-in café glowing warm against the cold, Frenchmen in blood-stained aprons drinking green liqueur and coffee at a zinc-topped bar.

Privilège
La Favorite

Poisson Arrivage
Filet de Merlu

I landed another client in Neuilly and did a few more dinners for Pierre and some in Switzerland, near where my mom lived. My fireplace apartment had become too expensive, so I moved to a tiny, soulless place in the 19th—white tile floors, narrow as a corridor.

The stress of the dinners was starting to get to me—the shopping, the packing, the hot Métro rides in rush hour with raw sweetbreads stuffed in side pockets. My window for success felt razor-thin. I carried everything I thought I didn't know into every dinner. Paris had devoured me and spit me out. I ambled through the city like a ghost, feeling forgotten and lost. I'd go to the Musée d'Orsay on Thursday nights, when it was free, and stay until closing. One night, crossing the river to the Right Bank, I saw an orange-and-pink harvest moon hanging low over a small bridge, covering its whole length. It was huge and dreamlike, and I thought about every woman I had ever loved. And I realized I was heartbroken, nostalgic, and tremendously lonely.

I learned that demis (half-sized beers) and baguettes got cheaper the farther you went from the heart of Paris, and I'd make a daily pilgrimage to Au Petit Fer à Cheval. It was my other home, a little brasserie in the Marais. It had green metal and glass doors that folded open onto the street, with tables and chairs facing out on either side of the entrance. There was a mosaic-tile floor and a marble-top horseshoe bar in the middle. Soft-brown tiles and white wainscotting ran along the walls, cracked with age. Big, ancient mirrors, marked and cloudy, lined both sides of the room. I'd order the plat du jour, and the chef would load up my plate. If you got there early enough, you could nestle into a side of the horseshoe and sit there for hours, watching people come and go and letting the honking bustle of Paris fall away.

The waiters wore black vests, white shirts, and aprons. Everything ran with ease and precision. You could get a sandwich at the bar—chicken poached in red wine, or jambon fromage on soft baguette with sliced cornichons. Even a Coca-Cola was an elegant ritual, served in a stemmed glass with ice, a lemon wedge, and a tall spoon to stir it. In the back was a small dining room with mahogany tables pushed together.

The menu was classic: steak frites, steak tartare, duck confit, andouillette, cheval salad, and the plat du jour. Everything came with pommes sautées—round, golden, crisp—and thin, buttery green beans.

I finally reached the point where I felt in my heart that there was nothing left for me in Paris. I was about to concede and leave when Natasha, one of the owners of Artisan Foods, asked me to go with her to Alba, in Piedmont, Italy, the land of truffles and Barbaresco. She was meeting a client there who grew microgreens, and she didn't want to spend the whole time alone with him, so I was to be a buffer. I agreed. We stayed in a small hotel just outside the town center and met Nico, the owner. We ended up drinking wine and talking with him all night about food. His uncle was a famous chef, and his father had a restaurant in Torino. Through the night's conversation, I felt myself surfacing from the trenches for the first time in a long while. Just being out of Paris, I felt like I could share what I was trying to do, reflect on what I had accomplished, and stop chewing on my failures.

Eight months later, I was back at Nico's hotel, cooking dinner on Monday nights for people coming from Milan to work at the Ferrero chocolate factory in Alba.

12:25
ACIE

TABAC
Le Progrès
TABAC

Swiss Train Ride

SERVES 2

BÉCHAMEL SAUCE
- 3½ oz (100 g) butter
- 1 Tbsp all-purpose flour
- 1 cup whole milk
- Salt

SANDWICHES
- 1 tsp duck fat (or butter)
- 4 slices good white bread (we use challah at Union)
- 6 slices ham
- 4 slices Swiss cheese (or Gruyère if you want it a little more authentic)
- Butter
- 2 eggs
- Salt and ground black pepper
- 1 tsp Dijon mustard
- Bread-and-Butter Pickles (page 280)

There was a time when my mom worked as a teacher in Switzerland. I'd go visit her every once in a while and stay for the weekend, or a week if I could. It was a 6-hour train ride from Paris. I'd be shattered when I arrived in the evening, after the hot, relentless grind of the kitchen, cigarettes, beer, traffic, and bars. Thankfully, her place had all the things a mom's place should have. Home-cooked meals and a fireplace. A radio playing in the kitchen. Nice furniture and a big, clean washroom with a bathtub. A bed with clean sheets. After 5 days or so, I'd feel refreshed and ready to get back.

On my way home one time, I bought a croque monsieur in the train car. It was kind of perfect in its simplicity. It had just the right amount of béchamel, cheese, and ham. Trashy, but really good. I ate it at the bar and looked out the window as trees and roads flashed by. I was an hour from Paris. I could feel the excitement rise inside me, planning where to go first from Gare de Lyon: have a demi at Baron Rouge, meet Chris at Au Petit Fer à Cheval for a steak and wine, have a cigarette. The memory has stuck with me. This train ride, eating that croque monsieur, with the anticipation of Paris and all its possibility and beauty fast approaching. The croque was simple and beautiful too, and didn't try to be anything more than it was.

MAKE THE SAUCE: In a small saucepan over medium-low heat, melt the butter. Whisk in the flour until it looks like wet sand. If it gets too clumpy, add more butter. If it's too wet and loose (not sandy), you need a little more flour.

Whisk in the milk. Don't leave it, because it'll burn on the bottom and leave flakes in the sauce. Keep whisking for 7 to 10 minutes on medium-low heat until it starts to thicken. If it thickens too quickly, add a little more milk so it's not gluey when it's finished. I like my béchamel sauce smooth and silky, not thick. It'll thicken a bit more as it cools, so plan for that. Season with salt to taste.

CONTINUES

Preheat the oven to 400°F.

PREPARE THE SANDWICHES: In a large frying pan over medium-low heat, heat the duck fat. Place two slices of bread in the pan and toast until golden on the bottom. Flip and, while toasting the other side, smear some of the béchamel sauce on top. When the other side is golden, flip again and smear béchamel sauce on top. Add three slices of ham on one piece and two slices of cheese on the other piece. Place the cheese-topped slice on top of the ham one. Transfer the sandwich to a baking sheet and repeat to make a second sandwich.

Bake for 6 to 8 minutes, until the sandwiches look alive and melty, with a sizzle.

While the sandwiches are baking, add a little butter to the pan and fry the eggs. The yolks should be runny, not medium. The yolk adds to the lushness and joy of it.

Transfer the sandwiches to individual plates. Place an egg on top of each sandwich. Finish with salt and pepper, a little mustard on the side, and pickles on top of the egg, right next to the yolk.

Warm Spinach Salad *with* Bacon and Chèvre Chaud

SERVES 4

BALSAMIC VINAIGRETTE

1 cup canola oil

1 Tbsp Dijon mustard

1 Tbsp balsamic vinegar

Salt and ground black pepper

SALAD

1 cup pecan halves, chopped

10½ oz (300 g) bacon slab, cut into small strips

2 slices crusty bread

1 garlic clove

Olive oil

4 slices Paillot de chèvre (about 7 oz/200 g total), cut ½ inch thick (or a local chèvre log cut into rounds)

2 bunches large leaf spinach

TABAC HACK

This salad works with baby spinach as well, but I highly recommend fresh large leaf spinach—it's sturdy enough to handle the heat of the warm vinaigrette.

I pulled this recipe from the Paris archives. It was a staple on the menu there. The warm vinaigrette on the fresh spinach, with the bacon and the chèvre toast, is a really nice combination. I added toasted pecans for a bit of crunch. This salad is best when you can get the big, wrinkled spinach leaves harvested in summer—they're tough enough to stand up to the warm vinaigrette without wilting to nothing. But regular all-season spinach works too.

Preheat the oven to 400°F. Line a baking sheet with parchment paper.

MAKE THE VINAIGRETTE: In a medium bowl, combine the canola oil and mustard. Slowly whisk in the vinegar until it becomes a creamy brown. Season to taste with salt and pepper. If it's too mild, add more vinegar. If it's too strong, add more oil. If it splits and isn't coming together, place 1 tsp mustard in a clean bowl and slowly whisk in the split vinaigrette. Once it's together, correct the flavor. It might need more oil if it's too tart, or more mustard if it's too loose.

MAKE THE SALAD: Spread the pecans on the prepared baking sheet and toast for 6 minutes. Remove the pan from the oven and preheat the broiler to high. Transfer the pecans to a plate to cool, leaving the parchment paper on the pan.

In a large skillet over medium heat, sauté the bacon until golden. Pour off about three-quarters of the fat. Reduce the heat to low, add the vinaigrette, and stir slowly for 1 minute. Remove from the heat and keep warm.

CONTINUES

Toast the bread, cut each slice in half, and place on the lined baking sheet. Rub the surface with the garlic clove and drizzle with a bit of olive oil. Place a slice of chèvre on each. Broil for about 3 to 4 minutes, until the cheese is softened and golden and smells delicious.

Place the spinach in a large bowl. Pour in the warm vinaigrette and toss with tongs until the spinach is coated. To plate, pile the dressed spinach in shallow bowls. Set the warm chèvre crostini on top. Scatter the toasted pecans around for crunch.

Norwegian Sushi

SERVES 4

BEET GRAVLAX

2 raw beets, peeled and roughly chopped

1-inch piece fresh horseradish, peeled

2 oz gin

1 cup white sugar

1 cup kosher salt

1½ Tbsp coriander seed

1½ Tbsp fennel seed

1½ Tbsp caraway seed

1 bunch fresh dill, chopped

1 side of salmon (1½ lb/700 g), tail removed (ask your fishmonger to cut it off)

4 Yukon Gold potatoes (or Russets), peeled and quartered

Salt

½ cup heavy (35%) cream or butter

Ground black pepper (use Brasserie Lipp pepper if you've got it)

1 tsp Galangal Glaze (page 287)

4 tsp grated fresh horseradish

Bread-and-Butter Pickles (page 280), to serve

My friend Chris came up with something like this for a dinner we did together. He called it Irish sushi, and we used raw salmon, horseradish mash, and a mushroom ginger glaze. This is my version, more suited for cooking at home. I use beet gravlax, so it feels more Norwegian. The hot mashed potato with the salty-sweet, lush gravlax is very comforting. The horseradish is the wasabi, the glaze is the soy sauce, the pickle . . . you get it.

PREPARE THE GRAVLAX: Blitz the beets and horseradish with the gin in a food processor until you've got a rough paste.

In a large bowl, mix together the sugar, salt, coriander, fennel, and caraway seeds. Add the beet-horseradish mixture and dill, and stir to combine.

Lay the salmon skin side down in a deep dish or tray. Spread the cure all over and coat both sides completely. Dump whatever's left right on top.

Cover and refrigerate for 3 days. Flip the fish once a day so both sides spend time in that pool of cure juice that starts forming. After the third day, it's ready. Rinse the fish under cold water to remove the cure and pat dry. Slice thinly. Store any leftover gravlax in the fridge for up to 7 days.

MAKE THE SUSHI: Place the potatoes in a large pot, cover with cold water, and let the water run briefly to rinse off some extra starch. Add 1 tsp salt. Bring to a boil and cook until the potatoes are very tender and just starting to break apart, about 45 minutes. Drain the potatoes, leaving about ½ inch of cooking water in the pot. This will help keep the mash moist and fluffy.

In a medium saucepan, warm the cream over medium heat. Add the potatoes and mash with a fork. It's okay if it's not perfectly smooth—that gives it a look closer to sushi rice. Season generously with salt and pepper.

CONTINUES

TABAC HACK

If you can't find fresh horseradish to grate, mix 1 Tbsp prepared horseradish into the mash.

Using a tablespoon, scoop small mounds of mash onto a serving plate, similar in size to sushi rice portions. Layer with a few slices of gravlax. Drizzle the galangal glaze around the plate and sprinkle the horseradish on top of the gravlax. Garnish with pickles.

SUHLS
ROPDU
NWRIEN
GAORND

Dinner Party Shrimp Tempura

SERVES 12 (AS A PLATTER)

DIPPING SAUCE

1 packet (0.35 oz/10 g) instant dashi

½ cup boiling water

½ cup soy sauce (I prefer Yummy House)

1 Tbsp mirin (I like Honteri brand)

TEMPURA

1 cup tempura batter mix (I prefer Nissin brand)

¾ cup soda water

Ice cubes

3 cups canola oil, for frying

1 bag (2 lb/900 g, 16 to 18 count) shrimp, peeled and deveined, tails on (try to find wild-caught)

The best way to wow dinner party guests is to deep-fry something right out of the gate. It scratches that "frites" itch early, so the rest of the meal doesn't feel like it's missing something. And you don't want to be deep-frying later, when pots are boiling and you're juggling the rest of the meal. It's a solo mission. Do it once and with focus, and then put the fryer away.

I used to open nights like this when I was cooking dinners in Paris, going to strangers' homes. It put the host at ease—like, "okay, this kid knows what he's doing"—and set the scene for what was coming next. The key is good-quality shrimp, whether fresh or frozen.

MAKE THE DIPPING SAUCE: In a small bowl, mix the dashi with the boiling water. Stir in the soy sauce and mirin. Set aside.

MAKE THE TEMPURA: Place the tempura batter mix in a large bowl. Pour in the soda water and whisk until a medium-thick batter forms. Add a few ice cubes (the colder the batter, the lighter the tempura will be) and whisk. We want a slightly thin batter. As the ice cubes melt, you may need to add a little more mix to keep the right consistency, because it will continue to thin out.

In a medium pot, heat the canola oil to 375°F. Drop in a bit of batter—it should pop and sizzle. If it sinks, wait for the oil to heat further.

Pat the shrimp dry with a paper towel so the batter will cling to them better. Hold a shrimp by its tail and dip it in the batter, then drop it straight into the oil. Fry four or five shrimp at a time, so the oil stays hot, for about 1 minute per batch, until golden and crispy. Transfer to a plate lined with paper towels to drain. Continue cooking in batches.

Serve the tempura on a tray, with the dipping sauce alongside.

Grey Owl Carbonara

SERVES 4

1 lb (450 g) spaghetti
1 tsp olive oil
1 cup diced pancetta or bacon
1 shallot, finely diced
1½ cups heavy (35%) cream
7 oz (200 g) Grey Owl goat cheese, divided
Salt (optional)
Good few cracks black pepper

TABAC HACK

Warm your bowls in a 200°F oven so the pasta hits the table piping hot. Hot food is half the battle won.

My friend Chris taught me a version of this dish when I started cooking on the line at his first restaurant. We ended up taking it to Paris, where it became our weekly "pâte du jour." It was a French-style carbonara, with cream, shallots, lardons, and a yolk nested in its shell on top. I started making a Grey Owl gnocchi at Union which people really loved. This is a combination of Chris's carbonara and that gnocchi. This dish is best done in one fluid dance. No stopping and starting.

Bring a large pot of heavily salted water to a boil. Add the spaghetti and cook according to package directions. Five minutes into cooking the pasta, start the sauce.

In a large pan, heat the olive oil over medium heat. Sauté the pancetta until golden, about 4 to 5 minutes. Add the shallot and sauté for 1 minute. Add the cream, bring to a simmer, and add half the Grey Owl. Stirring, cook for 30 seconds. Then take the sauce off the heat.

Drain the spaghetti, saving 1 cup pasta water. Add a small ladle of pasta water to the sauce. (Don't overdo it. Add just enough to loosen the sauce so it coats the pasta. It should come together smooth and glossy.) Add the spaghetti, give the sauce a good stir, then add a final touch of pasta water to bring it all together. Heat for 1 more minute. Taste it. Between the pasta water, pancetta, and Grey Owl, it might not need salt, but if it does, season with a bit.

Using tongs, grab one serving's worth of pasta and drop it in the center of a bowl, twisting as you release to form a sort of nest. (It's a solid plating technique that keeps the pasta tightly centered.) Do the same for each bowl.

Reheat any leftover sauce until it's steaming. Evenly spoon it over each serving. Portion the remaining Grey Owl and divide over each serving. Finish with a good hit of cracked black pepper. Serve immediately.

PALAIS DES
A PARIS

Pork and Shrimp Burger *with* a Duck Egg

SERVES 6

- 2¼ lb (1 kg) ground pork (a little fat in there is good)
- 10 whole shrimp (12 oz/340 g), peeled, deveined, and chopped
- 1 egg
- 2-inch nub fresh ginger, grated
- 1 heaping Tbsp chili paste with sweet basil leaves
- 1 Tbsp soy sauce
- 1 tsp Dijon mustard
- 1 tsp pure maple syrup
- Salt and ground black pepper
- 4 Tbsp duck fat or tallow, for frying (or canola oil works too), divided
- ½ lb (225 g) Chinese broccoli
- 1 tsp extra virgin olive oil
- 6 duck eggs (or regular large eggs)
- Galangal Glaze (page 287), for drizzling
- Habanero Sauce (page 288), to serve

Another banger from the archives of Sunday night dinners in Chinatown. I found this sweet basil chili sauce on the shelf one night and grabbed some frozen shrimp and ground pork. It's like a dumpling burger with a fried egg. I bring it back every once in a while at Union for lunch. That holy basil chili sauce is what makes it sing.

Preheat the oven to 375°F.

In a large bowl, combine the pork, shrimp, egg, ginger, chili sauce, soy sauce, mustard, maple syrup, and a pinch each of salt and pepper. Mix with your hands until the mixture is fully combined and sticky. If you stick the meat to your hand, flip your hand over, and it still sticks, the meat is fully combined.

Form into six patties, about 1½ inches thick. Press them slightly flatter than you think you should, as they tend to tighten up into balls while cooking. Season with salt and pepper.

Heat a large oven-safe skillet over medium heat and add 2 Tbsp of the duck fat. Once the fat is hot, cook the patties for 4 minutes per side. Transfer the skillet to the oven and cook for 5 minutes, until the internal temperature of the patties registers 165°F.

Meanwhile, bring a large pot of salted water to a boil. Add the Chinese broccoli and cook for 3 to 4 minutes, until just tender. Drain the broccoli, then toss it with olive oil, salt, and pepper, to taste.

While the patties rest in the skillet, heat a nonstick pan over medium heat. Add the remaining 2 Tbsp duck fat, aiming for a calm sizzle when you add the eggs—not that splattery, too-hot kind that burns the whites before the yolks have a chance to cook. Fry the eggs.

Place a few pieces of broccoli on each plate. Top with a patty and drizzle with galangal glaze. Finish each plate with a fried egg. Serve with habanero sauce on the side.

Hen Supreme

SERVES 2

- 1 Cornish hen (about 1½ lb/700 g)
- Salt and ground black pepper
- 7 oz (200 g) slab of smoked bacon (or thick-cut bacon)
- 1 cup sliced button mushrooms
- Olive oil, if needed
- 1 shallot, sliced or diced
- ½ cup chicken stock
- Scant ½ cup heavy (35%) cream
- ½ tsp pure maple syrup, to finish
- Squeeze of lemon juice or ½ tsp red wine vinegar or apple cider vinegar, to finish

Understanding the beauty of putting less on a plate is directly proportional to how many laps you've done around the cooking track. When I try to explain "less is more" to a younger cook, I always end up saying: "You just need more laps. You'll get it. With each pass, you gain force. Confidence then kicks in. You shed what's not needed and go straight to the heart of it." But you don't get it until you get it, so trust me, less really can be more.

In Paris, we'd get these beautiful plump yellow des Landes chickens. We'd break them down and use breast meat for this dish. The magic is the pan sauce at the end, made by deglazing the pan with the bacon, mushrooms, and shallots. Back then, I never felt good about cooking it. It seemed too simple. I wanted more flair. I hadn't been around the track enough to get it. Now it feels like comfort. Don't overthink it, lean into it—it's like a good movie from the 90s. Serve it with Pommes Sautées (page 187) if you want.

Flip the hen breast side down. Using a knife or kitchen shears, cut along the backbone to split it in half. One side will have a little more neck and spine. Trim that off so both halves are even. Season with salt and pepper, cover, and let it sit in the fridge for an hour.

Preheat the oven to 400°F.

Heat an oven-safe heavy-bottomed pan (cast iron works great) over medium heat so there's a sizzle. Place the hen halves, skin side down, in the pan and transfer to the preheated oven. Roast for 10 minutes, then flip and cook for another 10 to 15 minutes, until golden and cooked through and the internal temperature of the leg meat registers 165°F. Ovens and birds vary. Yours might need a few extra minutes, depending on size.

While the hen roasts, cut the bacon slab into two slices, then cut each slice into ½-inch "lardon"-sized pieces.

CONTINUES

Transfer the hen halves to a plate and let rest while you prepare the sauce. Keep the pan with all the drippings; this will be the sauce base.

Making the sauce should be one fluid crescendo, from right after the hens come out of the oven to the table. Set the pan over medium heat. Add the bacon and sauté for 2 to 4 minutes, until golden and the fat starts to render. Add the mushrooms and, if needed, hit the pan with a bit of olive oil. Sauté until soft. Stir in the shallot and sauté for about 30 seconds.

Deglaze the pan with the stock, scraping up the brown bits. Let it come to a boil and reduce slightly for a hot minute or so, then add the cream and let it all simmer together for 30 seconds. Finish the sauce with the maple syrup, lemon juice, and salt and pepper to taste.

Transfer the hen halves to serving plates and spoon the sauce over top.

Arlequin's Rabbit Dijonnaise

SERVES 4

1 whole rabbit (3 lb/1.4 kg) (see Tabac Hack)

Salt and ground black pepper

2 Tbsp olive oil and/or duck fat, plus more as needed

3 carrots, peeled and cut into 1-inch chunks

2 shallots, sliced

3 sprigs of thyme

1 tsp cornstarch

1 Tbsp water

1½ cups chicken stock

1 cup heavy (35%) cream

3 to 4 Tbsp smooth Dijon mustard

Home Frites, for serving (page 135)

I learned this old Arlequin restaurant dish from Chris when he was cooking there. I always think of the place when I make it. It was bistro-esque, with dark-red booths. Me sitting there with my mom and dad, sister and brother. Warm, soft lights. Wood wainscotting. Faded mirrors hugging us while we ate this dish: rabbit in a shallow bowl, in a vibrant yet soothing mustard sauce, thin-cut fries on the side. Think of all that when you start to cook it.

Don't let the need to butcher the rabbit hold you back from making this dish. You can ask your butcher to do it for you, or you can grab four hind legs, and that works great too.

To butcher the rabbit, start by cutting off the front legs, then the back legs. From the belly, there's a flap of meat on each side just below the loin—cut those off too and save them for stew. Cut each of the back legs in half, at an angle through the middle, so you end up with two even pieces. When you hit the bone, lift your knife and give it a good hack; it's a small bone, but rabbit bones like to splinter, so check the cut for any shards. Now cut the middle section, up to the ribs, into two large pieces or three smaller ones.

Preheat the oven to 375°F.

Season the rabbit pieces generously with salt and pepper. (Go heavy, like an old French cook.)

Heat a large, heavy-bottomed roasting pan over medium heat. Add the oil or duck fat (I like to use both). Working in batches, sear the rabbit pieces until golden on both sides, about 3 minutes per side. You want a healthy sizzle and golden color—no smoke, no burning. It's a balancing act between the heat and the rabbit. Transfer the rabbit to a plate.

CONTINUES

TABAC HACKS

Rabbits are surprisingly easy to butcher—it's as if their front legs are barely attached to their bodies. Just follow the seams where their legs meet the spine, then cut off the front and back legs. The front legs come right off if you slide your knife along the body, toward the head. Cut the middle into two or three big pieces.

If you've got time or the urge, you can brine the rabbit overnight (see Chicken, Hen, or Rabbit Brine, page 284). But it works great either way.

Add more oil or fat to the pan if needed. Add the carrots, shallots, and thyme and sauté for 3 to 5 minutes, until softened.

In a small bowl, mix the cornstarch with the water until smooth. Set aside.

Add the chicken stock to the pan and bring to a simmer, scraping up all of the good stuff from the bottom of the pot. When it starts to simmer, add the cream, followed by the cornstarch slurry.

Add the rabbit pieces back to the pan and cover with parchment paper. Roast for 50 minutes. When the rabbit comes out, if there's a little bit of splitting of the cream, that's okay because the mustard will help emulsify it again.

Stir the mustard into the sauce. (It likes a lot of Dijon, so don't be shy.) Taste as you go and adjust the salt and pepper if needed.

Divide the rabbit pieces among four plates and ladle the sauce overtop. Serve frites alongside.

Steak Haché Tabac-Style *with* Sauce au Poivre

SERVES 4

SAUCE AU POIVRE

1 Tbsp canola oil or duck fat

1 onion, finely diced

½ cup drained green peppercorns

1 cup port

1 Tbsp Better Than Bouillon chicken or beef base

1 cup heavy (35%) cream, plus more as needed

1 Tbsp Dijon mustard

½ tsp Galangal Glaze (page 287, optional)

STEAK HACHÉ

2 lb (900 g) lean ground beef

1 Tbsp Dijon mustard

1 Tbsp soy sauce

1 tsp pure maple syrup

Salt and ground black pepper

1 Tbsp duck fat

Tabacs are like the diners of Paris. Limited equipment, small kitchens, and simple lunch fare. But within the simplicity, there's a life to the food that feels impulsive and tasty (with a little trash and force to go along with it). Steak haché with fries is one plat du jour. It's utilitarian for the everyday Parisian coming in for a hot lunch, coffee, cigarettes, and lottery tickets. It doesn't try any harder than that, but it has a feeling. A spirit. A tastiness that shows someone back there cares. Every once in a while, you get lucky. This dish, this sauce—they're for the everyday. You don't labor too hard, and you enjoy them for what they are.

MAKE THE SAUCE: Heat a saucepan over medium heat. Add the oil, then sweat the onion and green peppercorns until the onions are translucent, about 3 minutes. Add the port and cook off the alcohol smell for a minute or two.

In the meantime, mix the bouillon with 1 cup water to make the stock. Add that to the pan and stir until the sauce comes together. Whisk the cream and mustard into the sauce for depth and character. Cook until the sauce is reduced by about one-third. Remove from the heat.

MAKE THE STEAK HACHÉ: In a large bowl, mix the beef, mustard, soy sauce, maple syrup, and a generous pinch of both salt and pepper until just combined. Form into four patties and season again with salt and pepper.

In a skillet over medium heat, warm the duck fat. Sear the patties for 5 minutes, then flip and cook for another 5 to 7 minutes for medium-rare. Transfer the haché to a plate.

Pour the sauce into the skillet and bring to a simmer. Taste and adjust the seasoning. If it's too salty, add an additional ¼ cup cream.

Plate the steak haché with the sauce spooned over top.

Apple Berry Crumble

SERVES 6 TO 8

CRUMBLE TOPPING

2 cups all-purpose flour

2 cups packed brown sugar

1½ cups quick-cooking rolled oats

½ lb (225 g) cold salted butter, cubed

APPLE BERRY FILLING

2 lb (900 g) apples (I like Cortland or Honeycrisp), peeled and cut into 1-inch pieces

1 cup frozen mixed berries

¼ cup white sugar

1 Tbsp fresh lemon juice

1 tsp pure maple syrup

Pinch of salt

Ice cream or whipped cream, for serving

TABAC HACK

If you have some rhubarb (about 1 cup), add it to your crumble with another 2 tsp of sugar, and omit the cornstarch because it will naturally thicken the fruit filling.

We used to make trays of this in Paris. We had a bustling lunch crowd, so it was on the prix fixe menu. It took me a while to get the ratio right. You want the crumble to form clusters of butter, oats, flour, and brown sugar. At first, it seems like it won't come together, but as you keep working it, it suddenly does. This version's with apples and berries, but you can swap in pears, or use both apples and pears.

Preheat the oven to 350°F.

MAKE THE TOPPING: In a large bowl, whisk together the flour, brown sugar, and oats. Add the butter and start working it through with your hands. It'll take about 10 minutes, but eventually it'll start to clump into little clusters.

MAKE THE FILLING: In another large bowl, combine the apples, berries, sugar, lemon juice, maple syrup, and salt. Stir it all around until everything is coated.

Spread the apple mixture evenly in a 9 × 13-inch baking dish. Scatter the crumble topping over the fruit in clusters.

Bake for 1 hour, until the fruit is bubbling around the sides and the topping is golden and crisp. (You may need 10 minutes more, depending on your oven.)

Serve warm with ice cream or fresh whipped cream.

BUT BUY
ROSES FLOU

Bistro Tarte Tatin *with* Mascarpone Crème Fraîche

SERVES 4

BLITZ PUFF PASTRY

2 cups all-purpose flour

¾ cup + 1 Tbsp cold butter

1½ tsp salt

1 tsp honey

1 tsp fresh lemon juice

½ cup cold water

TARTE TATIN

4 medium Golden Delicious or Honeycrisp apples

1 cup white sugar

2 Tbsp butter

1½ tsp pomegranate molasses

½ tsp vanilla extract

½ tsp salt

MASCARPONE CRÈME FRAÎCHE

1 cup crème fraîche or sour cream

1 cup mascarpone cheese

TABAC HACK

You can use store-bought puff pastry in a pinch.

I used to walk past a similar tarte tatin in Paris on my way to work every day. The little bistro had it sitting on a stand at the zinc-topped bar. It had a beautiful reddish plum-like hue that stuck in my taste imagination. They served it with a bright white crème fraîche. I spent years trying to emulate it, never quite sure how they got it so dark and plum-like, until one day I added pomegranate molasses to the caramel. The mascarpone mixed with crème fraîche is a quiet nod to my grandmother, who liked her apple pie with a slice of cheese.

First step is to prepare the puff pastry. It can all be done in a stand mixer. You will also need a rolling pin and some self-compassion and patience, because it takes a little folding and rolling and resting and folding and rolling. You get it.

MAKE THE PASTRY: In a stand mixer fitted with the paddle attachment, combine the flour, butter, salt, and honey. Mix on low speed until the butter is evenly distributed but still in large chunks. Add the lemon juice and cold water. Mix just until a dough forms, but don't overmix—you still want fairly large chunks of butter in the dough.

Turn the dough out onto a floured surface, flatten it, wrap it in plastic wrap, and chill for 30 minutes.

On a lightly floured surface, shape the chilled dough into a rough rectangle. Roll it out evenly, pressing from the center outward, until it's about ½ inch thick. The surface should look smooth but slightly marbled with visible streaks of butter. Dust with flour as needed to prevent sticking, lifting and turning the dough occasionally to keep the shape even.

CONTINUES

With the dough lengthwise, fold one short end in toward the center by about one-third. Fold the opposite short end over the first so it fully covers it (like folding a letter). Press lightly. The piece should be a thick, three-layer rectangle. Turn the dough 90 degrees. Roll it out evenly to about ½ inch thick. Repeat the fold—one short end into the center, then the other over top. Repeat this sequence once more, then wrap the dough in plastic wrap and refrigerate for 30 minutes.

After chilling, repeat the same rolling and folding process two more times, for a total of five folds. Wrap the dough again and refrigerate for another 30 minutes.

Preheat the oven to 400°F.

MAKE THE TARTE TATIN: Peel and core the apples. Slice each apple crosswise through the middle (across the equator) to create two equal halves. Set aside one apple half to use later for filling in the centers.

In an 8-inch cast-iron pan over medium heat, add the white sugar and ½ tsp water. Cook until it becomes a deep-golden-brown caramel, stirring occasionally. Add the butter and stir—it's going to bubble. Stir in the pomegranate molasses, vanilla, and salt to calm it down. Let cool slightly in the pan. Nestle the apple halves over the caramel, flat side down. Cut small pieces from the reserved apple half and tuck them into the centers to fill any gaps. Lay a piece of tinfoil over top.

Bake for 20 minutes until the apples are par cooked. Let the apples cool at room temperature in the pan for about an hour before you top with the pastry.

Roll out the dough on a floured surface into a 9-inch round. Drape it over the cooled apples, then tuck the edges down along the inside of the pan. Using a paring knife, cut a few small slits in the pastry to allow steam to escape as it bakes.

Bake for another 20 minutes, until the pastry is golden and crisp. Let cool for an hour or two, then invert onto a serving plate while still warm.

MAKE THE MASCARPONE CRÈME FRAÎCHE: In a bowl, using a spatula, fold together the crème fraîche and mascarpone until smooth.

Serve the tarte warm or at room temperature with a spoonful of the mascarpone crème fraîche alongside.

SES FLOUR

CHARBON
PIPER

Piedmont: Nico's Hotel

I arrived in the fall, when truffle season was starting, and Nico picked me up at the airport. Short and in his 50s, with silver and gray hair that hung past his ears, Nico had a handsome, slim face, a narrow nose, and eyes that squinted and got really small when he smiled. He wore glasses around his neck, and V-neck sweaters. Nimble on his feet and jovial, he would scrunch his face and grumble, his voice very low, when he was expressing how some Italians react to things.

We stopped at Nico's father's tavern in Torino on the way to Alba. When you opened the door, you saw a dark mahogany vestibule framed by woven wood columns. Leaves were carved into the wood across the top of the vestibule, and on the walls were black-and-white photos of protesters and police from the 1970s. A big, worn-out reservation book was splayed open on the dark wood counter. It felt like you were walking through a giant ancient tree. The warmly lit, spacious dining room had round clothed tables scattered around it, and windows covered with ivy.

Nico's father was over 80 and close to retiring, but was still holding court. He was short, with pure white hair, and had a kind, gentle force about him. You could tell he enjoyed feeding people and was proud of Piedmont and its food. Piedmontese food feels like it was created not in taverns but in people's homes and farmhouses and yards—some sort of magic conspiring with the rich earth that gives birth to the truffles.

First we ate carne cruda, a veal tartare with lemon and olive oil, and then bagna cauda, a pot of slow-cooked garlic anchovies served with vegetables. This was followed by agnolotti del plin, a pinched ravioli stuffed with shredded rabbit and served with butter and sage. Finally, Nico's dad rolled over a cart of bollito misto, a mix of boiled beef (blade, brisket, and tongue), plump, fleshy chicken, and cotechino sausage. The aromatic broth had star anise and a subtle sweetness, and there was a green sauce of parsley and anchovy, and a roasted red pepper sauce. During the meal, we drank a bottle of Barbaresco, and at the end we had a cheese from Bra made of sheep, cow, and goat milk. The cheese was milky white and soft, and the wine smelled like cherries and petrol. I was hooked, stunned, and excited. The food and wine felt bold and rooted and totally magical. The meal hit me like an unhitched wagon sailing down a dirt road, and shot me back to the doorstep of my grandparents' house and into their kitchen.

Afterward, Nico's dad sat down and explained how the food had been born from poverty. The region was so poor, they just used what they had. For flourish, he added that he'd had to walk 5 miles to school in the winter. He told me about old men making bagna cauda in cauldrons on a fire outside in the fall—along the hillsides after the garlic harvest—using big wooden spoons to slowly stir and emulsify the garlic, oil, and anchovies. I was captivated. And the green and brown and gray shades of the rolling hills reminded me of Grey County back home, where my father's farm was. He talked about the hail cannons the farmers would fire off throughout the day when a hailstorm was imminent, in a half-crazed attempt to shift the atmosphere and fate and protect their grapes from being pierced and shredded. And I felt like my own reckless attempts with vegetable gardens at the farm weren't so far off base. I wanted to get back there and roll around in the dirt and build mounds of soil, plant vegetables, chuck rocks in the garden, hunt rabbits, and make soft white cheese.

Before I left for France, I had been growing a lot of stuff in the garden and fighting the weeds and just playing with the soil, but had abandoned those efforts when my dad—scratching his head and looking confused—said, "I've never heard of putting rocks in a garden before." It zapped me of my confidence and spirit of exploration, and made me feel like an idiot. But here in Piedmont, in this tavern and with the bang of hail cannons resonating in my mind, I felt that my efforts were vindicated.

On the way to his hotel, Nico exclaimed, "Teo, what you have eaten is tremendous!"

"Tremendous"—that was one of his favorite words. We went through the whole meal and how my stomach was reacting to it: the boiled meats, the pasta, the bagna cauda ...

"It's tremendous," he said again. "My father makes good food, but it's not in this century."

Which was true, but the old tavern enchanted me and made me eager to get into the more modern osterias in the hills so that I could experience how the next generation had interpreted and grown from the roots of the taverns.

The plan for me was to help out at Nico's hotel while procuring a few stages at osterias in the small towns that scattered the foothills. For the first couple of weeks, we drove around to various places, eating and talking and looking for opportunities. Once, at a little spot up on the hillside, we ate a five-course dinner with a particularly memorable second course: a savory torte baked with squash and served with fonduto, a cheese sauce made with fontina cheese. I found the combination incredible and joyful and heartfelt. The fonduto took me back to my grandmother's kitchen, where she taught me how to make her cheese sauce, amongst many other dishes. This Italian food felt like a validation of the food I'd grown up with, and to have it here, in this magical place, amongst truffles—the most mysterious and amazing thing that comes out of the earth—and the best wines in the world awakened in me a belief that I did have cooking roots. The possibility of leaving that haunting imposter feeling behind was exhilarating.

Nico asked the chef's wife if I could do a stage there, and she said something in Italian and left. I asked Nico what she'd said, and he replied, "She said, 'Let me go ask the Bear.'" A big, intense-looking man came out in a chef's jacket and a blue apron and explained that he wasn't a teacher, and he just cooked simple food, "So, you know, I don't know," and the offseason was coming, "and you know." It was his kind way of explaining that I would be an intrusion into their lives. These were family-run places. Their kitchens were filled with aunts and uncles, and grandmothers and grandfathers, and sons and daughters. An osteria was an extension of the home, with the slow pace a family would have when cooking dinner for themselves.

The pace was on full display at a roadside tavern where we stopped for lunch on the way to Torino to shop for supplies. It didn't look like much from the outside, but the parking lot was full. Inside, wood floors, round tables, paintings on the walls. The windows were steamed from the boiling pasta water and shook as big trucks rumbled by. Plates and cutlery clattered, the muffled tones of people eating really good food. The kitchen was a nook off the dining room. A couple of grandmothers and aunts cooked pasta while daughters and nephews moved through the room, clearing, serving, washing dishes. It reminded me of the old French school posters showing restaurants—red-checkered tables, families, waiters leaning over them, the cashier, the bar, and swinging doors with round windows leading to the kitchen. The place looked as simple and effortless as life in those posters, intimate and tied to everyday family cooking.

After many failed attempts at getting me a stage, and with the offseason creeping in, Nico told me I could cook at his hotel on Monday nights, because everything else was closed on Mondays except for the pizzeria on the corner. There was a small kitchen with four electric burners and a small oven, used to make coffee and eggs and stewed apples and quince with cloves for breakfast.

That first Saturday, I went to the outdoor markets to shop for Monday dinner. It was fall, so there were a lot of root vegetables and winter greens and quince and artichokes and big, thick-stemmed cardoons. There were rabbits and ducks at a little shop too.

I hadn't cooked for Nico yet, and hoped I'd impress. He had once described a shaved artichoke salad, so I did that to start. I sliced the artichokes as thin as I could, squeezed lemon juice over them and sprinkled salt to cure and tenderize, then finished with grated garlic and shaved Pecorino. For the amuse bouche, I made salt cod arancini—fried rice balls—with lemon and aioli. I'd had arancini on an overnight ferry to Morocco once, and the experience had stayed with me like a good dream. I seared duck breast, sliced it, glazed it with a sticky reduced jus, and served it with braised and roasted cardoons. For the last course, I served rabbit Dijonnaise with pommes sautées, a dish I'd been making for my mother since my youth. I finished with a dessert of quince bread pudding. One of the guests said it was reminiscent of her grandmother's cooking, and I knew I had hit the mark.

I did those dinners every Monday for a few months, trying out dishes Nico described: an octopus terrine, Roman-style fried artichokes, the carpaccio his uncle made, and the bollito misto of his father's tavern. I was getting there, but I still fumbled and felt like I hadn't cracked it yet for myself. I still felt a need to be shown how.

Nico seemed to love giving me impossible challenges. Some days I thought he was full of it, and others I thought he really did know his stuff. One of my best and toughest nights was when he hastily sent me to his girlfriend's villa in the hills armed only with what looked like a treasure map—a wandering curved line with an X at the end—a beef shank, and a few white truffles. Nico's girlfriend was arriving from Milan after a long work stint, so it was to be a homecoming dinner for her. Nico and a few friends would join us later. Before I left, he described how to make a fonduto that didn't split—a traditional test for a new bride. The key was to let the cheese relax into the milk for a while at room temperature, then slowly, really slowly, stir them together on low, low heat for an hour.

By the time I left Nico's hotel it was dark, and navigating the cliff-side roads was harrowing. On top of that, I was expected to cook a three-course meal with ridiculous time constraints—a beef shank, the shin, is tough and needs to cook for a long time. As I drove, the pungent, earthy aroma of the truffles filling the truck, my first thought was "How the fuck am I going to roast a beef shank in time?" quickly followed by "Where the fuck is this place?"

The way I had learned to operate was to throw myself into situations and cook my way out, following my instincts and using fear to drive me to create something with heart and force. It was a way out of my head and into my heart, where I could *do* instead of constantly watching myself *be*. But sometimes fear and helplessness overwhelmed me and my inner critic kicked in. My parents had no faith in each other, and they were unable to foster self-belief in us kids. Cooking was my way of finding success and approval, but it was all I had. With no foundation of self-confidence to stand on, I could easily turn on myself.

So as I was driving, I really started to rip into myself. "How the fuck is that fontina going to melt with the milk and not split without cornstarch? You're really fucked now! Not to mention that you have no idea where you're going! You'd get lost in a mall!"

But I finally got there, with an hour and a half to get ready. After I took a few sips of beer and had a cigarette, and noticed wild herbs growing alongside the stone house, I went in and started to cook.

Beef in Piedmont is different. The cows are mostly grass-fed, and younger when they're killed, giving their meat a pinkish-red hue. I preheated the oven and got the shank ready to go in. My grandfather always hit beef with soy sauce, Worcestershire, garlic, and a lot of black pepper and salt, so I did the same, and also added olive oil and some rosemary that I'd picked outside. I nestled the shank on top of chopped onions, carrots, and leeks, and roasted it for 20 minutes at 400°F, then turned it down and put a little water in the roasting pan so the vegetables wouldn't burn (plus I figured the steam would help the shank get tender).

I grated the fontina into a pot with some milk and let it sit for as long as I could. After an hour or so, I anxiously and slowly warmed it, whisking the mixture while I thought about the bride having to do this in front of her new family. The fonduto split pretty quickly, so I strained it and started again, this time making a roux like my grandmother had taught me. That worked. Then I made some arancini to fry up when they arrived. I also had some Piedmont saucissons and fresh bread I'd got in the market.

They all arrived late, just as I was pulling the shank out of the oven. It was moist, tender, and gummy, and there was a glistening jus amongst the roasted vegetables, which had caramelized and burned a little at their tips.

The first course was the fonduto with shaved white truffle and a poached egg. I warmed the fonduto and added a little milk to thin it out, then poured it into bowls, dropped a soft-poached egg into each, and shaved a bundle of thin white truffle on top. I sat down as everybody started to eat. The room went silent, the smell of the truffles melting into the hot fonduto washing over us. Eating the dish felt like the roots of the earth were latching on to my brain and tingling my neurons. It was like nothing I had ever experienced before. It tickled my senses and brought new thoughts and feelings, like I was being given some secret knowledge of the earth. When we finished the dish, there was more silence, and I felt full of wonder and joy and thankfulness.

That dinner was the pinnacle of my time with Nico. It was all downhill from there. The hotel was slowing down in the offseason, and so was Nico's joyfulness and his enthusiasm for me—words like "tremendous" were slowly being replaced with *cazzo* and *bastardo* as the stress of a slow hotel got to him. My imposter syndrome crept in again, compounded by Nico's cold shoulder.

I had a small room in the attic with a cot and a skylight. I read a lot of Raymond Carver with the moon shining above me, and I dreamed of the neighborhoods he wrote about and the struggling couples who lay on couches and drank too much at dinner parties.

A friend of mine from Boston was in Milan for a few days; we had been roommates when I was cooking at my uncle's diner in Watertown. So, feeling unwanted, I hopped on a train. As the rolling hillsides flew past my window, I dug deep into my failures: I'd never gotten a stage at an osteria, my Italian still sucked, I hadn't really learned how to make authentic Italian carne cruda, or bollito misto, or bagna cauda, or fonduto. But as I thought about those dishes, it occurred to me that I knew how I *wanted* them to taste. And somewhere amongst the gray-green fields, between the cages filled with drying corn and the three prawn trees that had been trimmed down to their knuckles, it all just cracked open. I *did* know how to cook those dishes. I could imagine how I wanted a dish to be and taste, and no one could teach me what I already knew. I could figure it all out from the inside. The spell of disappointment—the weight of everything I didn't know—had lifted.

When I returned to the hotel from Milan, I knew I wouldn't be staying there much longer. I left early one morning in late spring. I was meeting my father and brother, and we were going to drive along the coast. I had my knapsack on, ready to catch the first train. Nico was at the desk, and he let me have it.

I walked out the door. There was a mist in the air, and dew everywhere, and I could smell sage and the earth as I walked up the road to the train station. I was shaken. My time in Alba may have looked like a failure to Nico, as it once had to me, but I knew now that it wasn't. I knew it. I clung to my epiphany and tried to see past Nico's outburst. Looking back now, I think he was hurt and sad to see me go.

From that time on, I didn't feel like an imposter anymore, and that meant everything to me. My stay in Italy, and the work I did there, opened me up to cooking from the inside—creating dishes based on my style and what I imagined food to be. That way of cooking felt limitless. I had a whole new journey ahead of me.

Bagna Cauda Beefsteak Tomato Salad

SERVES 4

BAGNA CAUDA

12 garlic cloves

¾ cup canola oil

10 salted cured anchovy fillets

¼ cup water

Squeeze of lemon juice

Salt

TOMATOES

4 beefsteak tomatoes (big, ripe, and beautiful)

Salt

½ tsp sugar

FOR SERVING

Extra virgin olive oil, for drizzling

Ground black pepper

Fresh basil leaves

Toasted baguette

In Piedmont during the fall, you'll find old guys with cauldrons in the hillsides making big batches of bagna cauda—a stewed garlic and anchovy sauce—when the garlic is harvested. The area was historically poor, and this was a hearty source of winter protein. It all adds to the magic of the region, along with the hail cannons they fire and the truffles buried underground.

When I was a kid in Ontario, during the late summer at my grandparent's cottage, dinner always included a platter of peeled beefsteak tomatoes, sliced and salted, with a little sugar. My grandparents would pick up tomatoes at the farm stand, along with fresh corn for dinner. This dish is a combination of Piedmont and Ontario, of my grandparents and the grandfathers on the hillside.

MAKE THE BAGNA CAUDA: In a small saucepan over low heat, confit the garlic in the canola oil until golden and soft, about 15 minutes. Strain the garlic from the oil, reserving both.

While still warm, blend the garlic with the anchovies and water in a high-speed blender or food processor. With the motor running, slowly stream in the warm confit oil to emulsify into a smooth sauce. Add the lemon juice and salt to taste.

BLANCH THE TOMATOES: Bring a large pot of water to a boil and set up an ice bath nearby. Using a small knife, gently score an X on the bottom of each tomato (this is where you'll peel the skin after blanching).

Place the tomatoes, two at a time, into the boiling water and blanch for 20 to 30 seconds—you don't want to cook them, just loosen the skin. (Resist blanching all four tomatoes at once, as it will lower the water temperature.)

CONTINUES

Using a hand strainer, transfer the tomatoes to the ice bath and blanch the other two tomatoes. After about a minute in the ice bath, remove the tomatoes. The skins should peel off easily.

Once peeled, cut out the cores and slice the tomatoes into ½-inch-thick rounds. Arrange on a platter, season with salt and sugar, and let them sit for 20 minutes before serving.

TO SERVE: Arrange the tomatoes on a platter and drizzle generously with the bagna cauda. Finish with a drizzle of olive oil and some pepper. Fresh basil is great here, and some toasted bread too.

Italian Ferry Arancini

MAKES 20 ARANCINI

SEAWEED STOCK

1¾ oz (50 g) dried wakame

1 strip (¾ oz/20 g) dried kelp (kombu)

ARANCINI

1 Tbsp olive oil

1 onion, diced

1 lb (450 g) Carnaroli rice

2 cups Tomato Soup (page 101) (or 1 can Campbell's tomato soup + 1 can water)

2 cups grated Piave cheese

Salt and ground black pepper

1¾ oz (50 g) Taleggio or soft sheep cheese, cut into 1-inch cubes

PASTELLA

1 cup flour

2 cups Seaweed Stock

1 egg, beaten

2 cups Italian breadcrumbs

3 cups canola or sunflower oil, for frying

When my cousin Tim and I were 19 and 20, we took an overnight ferry from Italy to Morocco, heading for Essaouira to see Jimmy Hendrix's castle made of sand—an old Portuguese fort built too close to the sea. We ended up staying there for 3 weeks.

On the ferry, there was a snack bar serving tomato arancini balls. They were golden, crisp, and comforting as we journeyed across the sea at night, sleeping on the floor with our backpacks under our heads. Years later at Union, I realized the tomato soup I had developed there brought back that flavor memory. I decided to use a seaweed stock of dried kelp and wakame to cook the risotto halfway, then finish with tomato broth. It felt right, like the rolling sea was underneath me all over again.

MAKE THE SEAWEED STOCK: In a medium pot, simmer the wakame and kelp in 4 cups of water, covered, for about 10 minutes (the seaweed will expand in the stock, so you may need to add more water). You want the stock to taste like the sea. Strain and set aside.

COOK THE RICE: In a heavy-bottomed shallow pot, heat the olive oil over medium heat. Sweat the onion for a few minutes, until golden. Add the rice and stir to coat.

Add 2 cups of the seaweed stock and the tomato soup. Bring to a boil, give it a good stir, then reduce the heat to medium-low, cover, and let simmer for 10 to 15 minutes, until the liquid has evaporated. Stir toward the end to make sure it hasn't burned; the rice should be a little al dente.

While the rice is cooking, chill a baking sheet in the freezer. Once the rice is cooked, gently spoon it onto the tray and grate the Piave evenly over the top. Season with salt and pepper, then leave to cool in the fridge for about 1 hour.

CONTINUES

FORM THE ARANCINI: To "nonna" it, flatten a scoop of rice in your palm, place a Taleggio cheese cube in the middle, fold the rice over it, and form into a tangerine-sized ball. (Be mindful of size—if the balls are too big, they will brown quickly without getting warm in the middle.)

COAT THE ARANCINI: Once the rice balls are stuffed and ready, make the pastella: whisk the flour with the remaining 2 cups seaweed stock and the egg until smooth. The mixture should resemble a light batter.

Dip each rice ball into the pastella, letting any excess drip off, then roll in the breadcrumbs to coat.

Heat the canola oil in a large, heavy-bottomed pot—enough oil to submerge the balls, about 4 to 5 inches deep. Aim for 375°F. If you don't have a thermometer, drop in one ball. If it sizzles gently, you're good.

Add a couple more balls to the pot, but don't crowd it (too many balls at once will drop the temp too much, and the arancini will come out soft and greasy). Fry the balls for about 4 minutes, until golden brown and crispy. Transfer to a paper towel–lined plate. Repeat until all of the arancini are cooked.

Allow the arancini to cool before digging in (they taste better once they cool a little).

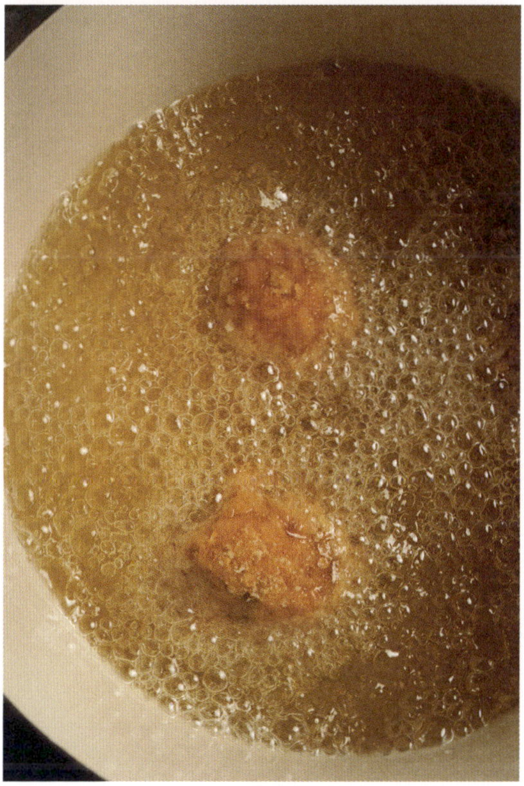

Gnocchi Bolognese

SERVES 6

BOLOGNESE SAUCE

2 Tbsp olive oil

2 lb (900 g) ground beef

1½ lb (700 g) ground bacon (see headnote)

1 onion, diced

2 garlic cloves, grated

1 Tbsp Korean ground red pepper (gochugaru)

1 Tbsp Kingsgate Reserve fortified wine (or any fortified wine)

2 Tbsp heavy (35%) cream

1 Tbsp soy sauce

1 Tbsp pure maple syrup

Salt and ground black pepper

1 can (28 oz/796 mL) whole Roma tomatoes

4 cups tomato passata

1 bay leaf

GNOCCHI

3 medium potatoes

Salt

2 egg yolks

1¾ oz (50 g) Piave cheese, grated, plus more for serving

Pinch of ground nutmeg

1 cup 00 flour, plus more for dusting

Semolina, for dusting

When I first opened Union, my friend Alex worked in the basement during the day, prepping food and butchering for his own prepared-food business. One of the things he made was a Bolognese sauce, and we adopted it at Union. It became the perfect way to use up leftover tartare, burgers, and sliders, and the bacon slab ends left over from slicing. The ground bacon gives the sauce its smokiness—ask your butcher to grind it for you. There might be too much Bolognese for your gnocchi, but it freezes well.

MAKE THE SAUCE: In a large, heavy-bottomed pot over medium heat, warm the oil. Add the beef and bacon and cook for 7 to 10 minutes, stirring occasionally, until the beef starts browning. Add the onion, garlic, and Korean pepper and sauté for 5 minutes.

While stirring, add the fortified wine and let it cook off for 3 minutes. Stir in the cream and cook for another 3 minutes. Stir in the soy sauce, maple syrup, and salt and pepper to taste.

Meanwhile, tip the canned tomatoes into a bowl and crush them with your hands. Add them to the pot, followed by the passata. Add a splash of water to each can and the jar to get every bit, and pour that into the pot too. Bring to a simmer and add the bay leaf. Partially cover so the steam can escape and simmer over low heat for 1 hour, stirring occasionally. Remove the lid and cook for an additional 30 minutes. Discard the bay leaf. Taste and adjust the salt.

Preheat the oven to 450°F.

MAKE THE GNOCCHI: While the sauce is simmering, start in on the gnocchi. Stab the potatoes a few times with a fork. Arrange them on a bed of salt on a baking sheet and bake for 1 hour or until fork-tender (you might need an extra 5 minutes). Let cool slightly, until you can handle them, then peel.

CONTINUES

Dust your work area with flour. Rice the potatoes directly onto the surface, forming a mound. Make a well in the center and add the egg yolks, Piave, nutmeg, and 1 tsp salt. Add ¾ cup of the flour and use a bench scraper to chop it into the potatoes. Begin working the dough, adding more flour until it's no longer sticky (about 1 cup total).

Cut the dough into eight pieces. Dust your work area with semolina and roll each piece into a rope. Cut into 1-inch-sized pieces.

To serve, cook the gnocchi in a large pot of salted boiling water until they float, just for a minute or two. Drain well, reserving ½ cup of pasta water.

Ladle about 3 cups (that's six soup ladles) of the Bolognese into a large pan. Warm it over medium-low heat, then add the cooked gnocchi and a little bit of pasta water. Toss gently and cook for 1 minute. Plate and finish with grated Piave.

Galangal Braised Beef Shin *with* Root Vegetable Mash

SERVES 6

- 1 whole beef shin (about 4 lb/1.8 kg), cut in osso buco pieces
- Salt
- 2 tsp ground black pepper
- 1 Tbsp duck fat or olive oil
- ½ cup red wine (optional if you don't have it around)
- 1 can (14 oz/398 mL) whole Roma tomatoes
- 2 onions, halved and sliced
- 1 big nub of galangal, peeled and chopped
- 1 cup water (or beef/chicken stock)
- ½ cup soy sauce (I like Yummy House brand)
- 1 Tbsp brown sugar

ROOT VEGETABLE MASH

- 3 tennis ball–sized rutabagas, peeled and quartered
- 2 turnips, peeled and quartered
- 4 Yukon Gold or Russet potatoes, peeled and quartered
- 1 tsp salt, plus more to taste
- 1 Tbsp butter or olive oil, plus more to taste
- Ground black pepper

This dish goes back to a hillside in Piedmont. Nico gave me the beef shin and sent me up the hill to his girlfriend's place with a white truffle and some loose instructions on how to cook it. I got lost. Had a meltdown. Then pulled myself together enough to make a fonduta with truffle and braised beef shin. It's one of my fondest cooking and eating moments, hands down.

We started making this version at Côte de Bœuf when we were bringing in beef hips for tartare and piling up beef shins.

Preheat the oven to 400°F.

Season the shin pieces generously with salt and the black pepper. Heat a heavy-bottomed oven-safe pot or a roasting pan over medium heat. Add the duck fat and sear the meat until you've got a deep golden crust.

Add the wine to deglaze the pot, scraping up the brown bits. Then add the tomatoes, onions, galangal, water, soy sauce, and brown sugar. Give it a good stir.

Cover the pot with foil and roast in the oven for 1 hour, until the beef is falling off the bone and smells amazing.

MAKE THE MASH: Meanwhile, rinse the rutabaga, turnip, and potato pieces quickly under cold water to knock off some starch, then toss them in a large pot. Fill the pot with water, pouring a bit off the top so it doesn't boil over. Add the salt, bring to a boil, and boil for 45 minutes, until everything is soft and slightly breaking apart.

CONTINUES

TABAC HACKS

With root vegetables, I try to go organic. They're sweeter and just taste better. Good soil makes a big difference.

Root mash is awesome if you can get your hands on some good tallow—sub it for the butter.

Drain the vegetables, saving 1 inch of cooking water to help the mash come together. Return the veg to the pot and add the butter. Mash the veg, then fold through with a spatula. Season with salt and pepper to taste. You might need more butter too.

Spoon the mash into the middle of a large bowl, set the beef on top, and pour some sauce over it.

GE LIQUOR

UNION

Union

Union

While I was in Italy, I had heard about an up-and-coming strip back in Toronto, on Ossington Avenue, and thought it would be a great place to open a restaurant. I had just enough confidence to do something big, and was naive enough to think it was a good idea. If people knew how difficult opening a restaurant is, there wouldn't be any restaurants. But I was excited by the idea, and so was my dad. He wanted to invest and help me build it. While we were in Italy, eating fritto misto by the sea, he came up with the name: Union. We talked about what it might look like, and the style of food I'd serve.

When I got home to Toronto, we went together to see the space. Ossington was still rundown, a high-danger zone of Vietnamese gangs and karaoke joints. A double murder had taken place in a bar just down the street. But the area was also slowly turning over and getting gentrified. The place we were looking at was one of many karaoke spots, a ramshackle shoebox with a couple of washrooms in the basement and dirt floors on the other side of the washrooms. It stunk like mold and had an ugly red paint on the walls and black-tinted windows in the front.

We had a bank loan and a credit card. My father took out a line of credit and invested a huge sum to get us to the finish line. I had no idea what I was doing. All I knew was I wanted a horseshoe bar in the front. I wanted it to be just like my favorite spot in Paris—Au Petit Fer à Cheval—where you'd be greeted right away by the bartender and feel a welcoming ease when you stepped in for a drink or a coffee. And like

Au Petit Fer à Cheval, the dining room would be nestled behind the partition of the bar. I wanted to have an open kitchen so cooking wouldn't feel like work but instead like I was entertaining friends. Plus, I wanted to feel the energy of the place while I was on the line. The project was totally faith- and family-driven, and I hoped to replicate the spirit of a family-run tavern.

I gutted the place with a few friends. It had been put together haphazardly, so it broke down easily, exposing good bones—brick walls and tall ceilings. I thought, "Oh, this is not so bad." The basement was a challenge; the floors were warped and moldy because they'd been laid down on dirt. I ripped up the cheap plastic linoleum tiles and started to dig so there'd be enough ceiling clearance for a concrete floor, carrying out the dirt in buckets. I spent a week or so on my own, lugging buckets of dirt up the stairs. My mom and her friend came by during this time, the upstairs stripped down, with wood and wires hanging and broken windows, and me, filthy and exhausted. My mom's friend looked around and said, "Oh, you poor thing." And it caught me by surprise. You just don't see how deep a hole you have dug for yourself is while you are in it, and there's a grace there that allows you to push and claw your way through the darkest moments.

Every contractor and tradesman in the beginning was terrible. I actually believed they cared about my vision for the place, but they turned out to be a string of crappy tradesmen who preyed on my clouded state of enthusiasm and naivety. I was writing a blog for a magazine about opening Union, so I would sit on the floor and write while I waited for an electrician or a plumber not to show up. All of the failures made for an interesting story. But fundamentally, I knew that if I could build this spot, I could make the restaurant happen as I'd hoped. And eventually I found good people who rescued me, and soon enough, the marble-topped horseshoe bar went in, along with a marble-topped chef's bar at the back and subway tiles in the kitchen.

What I cherish from this period is the time spent with my father, searching for tables and sinks and mirrors, bidding on stuff at auctions, whatever we could rummage up for the decor. We got a giant antique mirror by jumping in at the very last second to top a bidding war; it was all him, and it was stealthy. We'd pillage barns for sinks and countertops and doors. We found lights from old department stores at dusty antique shops. We nabbed door frames and mailboxes and silver serving utensils and neon signs. The places we went to find all that stuff are mostly gone now, like the city was coughing up its last relics, adding to my sense that it was a very special time.

It was exciting, thinking about the place and hashing out ideas, and my father and I had a bond going like good friends. He opened up and confessed that he suffered from depression (mild, as he put it, but that was always his way of delivering news: in the best light possible.) He was on antidepressants, and for the first time, he seemed happy, less wounded and constrained and discouraged. My childhood is thick with memories of him spending a long time in bed on weekends. When we did play catch, or when he'd throw for batting practice, it was always quick and felt burdensome. As a kid, I took that to mean I wasn't really worth his time. Now he was different—engaged and enthusiastic. He seemed energized, and was a lot less grumbly and head-scratchy and frustrated by little things. I almost felt like we were best friends, bonded by the effort, the grit, the shared drive to get it right.

When the build-out of Union was finally finished, the place had hemlock floors, the horseshoe bar, and an open kitchen with a chef's bar. Barbara Klunder, a well-known artist and family friend, did a massive mural on one side of the restaurant depicting a horse racing out of a barn amidst barrels and seagulls and bees and grass. We hung the antique mirrors on the brick walls across from the mural. My friend Josh made the lights. His father was a theater architect, and Josh talked a lot about sparkle and warmth. He built large steel three-armed pieces with globes at the ends, as if the lights were suspended in the air, which gave off a beautiful, warm glow throughout the dining room. The open kitchen, with its marble chef's bar wrapped around it, had a big flat-top with two ovens, a deep fryer, and an old black Garland six-burner with

UNION

an oven. The Garland was the one thing (along with the liquor license) that we salvaged from the old Vietnamese karaoke place.

We intended to eventually open the backyard as an outdoor patio, but on opening night it was still full of rubble and dirt and weeds and broken glass. I parked my dad's 1967 red Ford pickup there that day, sat on the tailgate, and took my best shot at a menu. My idea was that the menu would change every night, built around the best produce and meat available—the classic farm-to-table model. But five of the dishes I came up with that day, while sitting on the tailgate of my dad's truck, are still on the menu, and everything else changes around them. All of these dishes reflect a part of me, inspired by my travels—the tavernas in Italy and brasseries in Paris—and rooted in my grandparents' cooking.

I had a Union salad, inspired by the chèvre salad at Au Petit Fer à Cheval, but with a touch of honey and black pepper on a scoop of soft chèvre, served with double-smoked bacon, a rösti, and green and butter lettuces. The steak tartare was inspired by the carne cruda in Piedmont. I did it with a vibrant, lemony organic olive oil from Spain, mixed with French-style tartare touches, adding a little soy sauce and Dijon mustard for depth and topping it with my grandmother's bread-and-butter pickles. It's served with toast, smeared with duck fat and seared on the flat-top, using cornbread from the Portuguese bakery down the street. I had sticky ribs—an ode to Mickey's Ribs, a little takeout rib joint that was around the corner from my house in the 1980s; I can still remember eating ribs on my parents' bed while watching a small TV. I finished the ribs on the barbecue out back with a sticky, sweet-sour barbecue sauce, just like Micky did. I did a steak haché au cheval, a burger with an egg on top, which was a staple in the tabacs and brasseries in Paris (it's not actually made of horse, but has *cheval* in its name because the yolk resembles a horse's eye—at least, that's what my Belgian friend Johan told me). I also had steak frites, the steak marinated as per my grandfather's instruction with soy and garlic and a ton of black pepper, and the frites served with aioli.

I also did haddock cakes, made with fish from a family-run supplier out of the East Coast, with celery salt and aioli and seaweed salad, along with a few family-style platters: a whole roasted chicken, sourced from a lady near my farm, and a côte de bœuf that became something of a signature.

We got good reviews and were busy. But pretty quickly, the place became a runaway train. I had no idea how to run the business side of things, and the people I trusted to do it just didn't. Then, one terrible, hot Saturday night, I was cooking on the line. I hadn't heard from my father that day, which was unusual, but I brushed it off and kept prepping for dinner. As time went on, however, a sinking feeling grew in my gut that would not let up. I just knew something was wrong. I walked off the line in the middle of service, got in my pickup truck, and drove to his apartment, with the ballgame on to distract me from my fear. When I was a kid, I would check on my dad when he was sleeping, like he was a baby, to see if he was breathing. Now, when I got to his apartment and called out to him, there was no answer. I walked around the corner, and there he was, lying face down on the parquet floor. He'd had a massive heart attack that had stopped him in his tracks.

What followed was one of the worst times of my life. I was operating in a state of shock and grief and fear beyond measure. My father—a central force in my life—was gone. He was one of the main reasons the restaurant even existed. But his death brought to light that his finances, of which my restaurant was a big part, needed cleaning up. I felt a tremendous amount of sympathy for him, to have been yanked from the world like that. I couldn't let his investment be for nothing. I couldn't let my restaurant become a stain on his name. It wouldn't be easy, and there were no guarantees, but I was determined to make the restaurant work and dig it out of the debt it was in.

Over the next weeks, I had a crash course on all aspects of the business—front and back. I learned how cash moved through the bank, how to pay taxes monthly, how to reconcile the books and read a balance sheet. I called every unpaid supplier to let them know what had happened and that their money was coming. Deep down, I knew that if I could run this place my way and cook the way I knew how, I could make it work. I just needed enough runway to get off the ground. Most of the time, I was terrified. Shattered. But on the line, I cooked in the moment, as if my life depended on it.

Slowly, I started to execute what I believed in. Both staff and guests showed up who understood my vision. When I trained someone on how to dress a salad, I would say, "Imagine you're an old Frenchman making salad for his family. You know what I mean?" When describing how to make smashed potatoes, I'd say, "They should taste like you're sitting on the veranda with your grandmother, looking at the lake in the summer." What I was trying to say was: Cook like your family is out there in the restaurant. Cook with strength, conviction, and force, because the food will be more vibrant and alive that way. Often, I was greeted with a blank stare, and they'd move on to some other place. But some people got it.

I didn't have any real structure. It was by-the-seat-of-your-pants kind of cooking, but it had its moments. Looking back, it's a blur, like it was on high speed all the way through. But our finances started to improve. Slowly. A bit of luck and good timing—that's what got me through the first few months. Landing a huge catering job was the final chunk of cash that got our books settled up. (Although I nearly burned the place down when a lamb caught on fire on the barbecue—but I pulled it off.)

I'd like to think I could have made Union a success if my father had still been alive, but I don't think that's true. It took his death to shake me out of my complacency and force me to become an adult. That truth still sits heavy.

Union Breakfast Sandwich

SERVES 1

- 1 tsp duck fat (or more, depending on how you're feeling)
- 1 Rösti (page 105)
- 2 slices challah or doughy white bread
- 2 tsp Spicy Mayo (page 286)
- 1 large egg
- Salt and ground black pepper
- 2 slices ham (prosciutto cotto or Black Forest)
- 1 slice Swiss cheese
- 1 leaf green lettuce (butter, romaine, green leaf—whatever you prefer)

I came up with this recipe after the lady who runs Bang Bang Ice Cream & Bakery, across the street from Union, told me to make an egg salad sandwich with a fried rösti inside. She's good at what she does, so it stuck in my head, and I tried it one morning at Union.

It's easy to prepare this sandwich on a flat-top and with a deep fryer, but you can pull it off at home by making it the Swiss way—a pan-fried version. The spicy mayo, lettuce, and crispy rösti give it a McDonald's flavor without that fleeting feeling. You can use one pan, either nonstick or cast iron, if it's big enough. It's like a crescendo of cooking that all comes together in a grand finale.

Heat a skillet or nonstick pan over medium heat. Add the duck fat and press the rösti down into the pan. Shallow fry for about 5 minutes, until golden and crispy, then flip and fry the other side. Remove the rösti from the pan.

Add the bread to the skillet and grill until golden on both sides, adding a little more duck fat if needed. Transfer to a plate and smear spicy mayo on the insides of each slice of bread.

Crack the egg into the skillet and cook sunny-side up until almost set. Flip it over-easy style—you can break the yolk a bit so it is not too runny. Season with salt and pepper. Place the egg on one slice of bread.

Stack the ham slices in the pan and top them with the Swiss cheese. Cook for about 1 minute, until the cheese melts slightly. Place the ham and cheese on top of the egg.

Top with the crispy rösti and lettuce. Close the sandwich up and slice in half.

Pancakes *with* Grated Apple

SERVES 6

- 2 cups all-purpose flour
- 2 heaping tsp baking powder (see Tabac Hack)
- 2 tsp brown sugar
- ½ tsp baking soda (for good luck)
- ½ tsp salt
- 3 large eggs
- 1¼ cups whole milk (or soy/nut milk for dairy-free)
- ½ cup water
- 2 tsp white vinegar
- 1½ tsp pure vanilla extract
- 3 Tbsp butter (or sunflower oil), plus more for cooking and serving
- 2 apples, peeled and grated
- Pure maple syrup, for serving

TABAC HACK

Check the expiry date on your baking powder and baking soda. If they're old, they lose their magic.

My dad spent about 40 years tinkering with this recipe. Sometimes he used bacon fat and vinegar instead of butter and lemon juice. Sometimes grated pears instead of apples. My fondest memory of warmth and love as a kid is being at the farm with him, making pancakes and bacon on the wood-burning stove. I'd grab a few apples that had rolled right up to the kitchen door from the big old apple tree up the hill. I'd quickly grate them and put a little pile on the pancake as one side cooked on the skillet. He'd say, "It ain't called a 'pan cake' for nothing," while pointing at how tall it was rising on the griddle. My dad would serve these with scrambled eggs and bacon—it was his ultimate breakfast.

If there's one thing I've learned after all these years at the griddle, it's that some batches, like some days, turn out better than others.

In a large bowl, whisk together the flour, baking powder, brown sugar, baking soda, and salt.

In a separate bowl, whisk together the eggs, milk, water, vinegar, and vanilla. Pour the wet ingredients into the dry and stir and fold gently. Don't whisk—just stir and fold with a spatula.

Melt the butter in the same large pan you're going to cook the pancakes in. Pour the melted butter into the batter, folding it in smoothly. Let the batter sit for 5 to 10 minutes to activate.

Heat your pan over medium heat—not smoking, just a good steady heat. Drop in some batter with a ladle or large spoon, about the size of a sand dollar. I do two or three at a time, depending on the size of the pan. When air bubbles form on the top, add a heap of grated apple on top, then flip. Cook for about 1 minute on that side, then slide the pancakes onto a warm plate in a 200°F oven to keep warm until the rest are ready. Melt more butter as needed between batches and repeat with the remaining batter and apple.

Serve the pancakes with butter and maple syrup.

Frittata *with* Sour Cream and Pickled Jalapeños

SERVES 6

2 Tbsp olive oil (or more, if needed)

1 cup mushrooms (I like shiitake, but button work), stemmed and roughly diced

1 onion, diced

1 cup blanched and finely chopped curly kale

Salt and ground black pepper

18 large eggs

1 scant cup heavy (35%) cream

Finger-sized chunk of Piave (or whatever cheese is in the fridge), grated

Sour cream

Pickled Jalapeños (page 282)

When I first opened for brunch at Union, it was just me on the line, one server, and a bartender. I made postcards that said "f@#$ brunch" and handed them out with the bills at night. I hired an oyster shucker named Tony, who went by the name Oystertaker. He was goth, had long black hair, and called oysters "bivalves" a lot.

I was hoping to recreate the vibe from the Baron Rouge in Paris—people hanging out all day, crushing oysters, drinking wine and champagne. All I wanted to do was put together a few charcuterie boards and poach an egg once in a while. That never happened. But I tried, hard. For a minute, we had live music. One week it was a trumpet player; the next, a saxophone player. It all peaked one spring Sunday when a clarinet player showed up. He pulled an ancient clarinet from its ragged case and started blowing. What came out sounded like death moans and screeching alley cats. A combination of panic and despair hit me. I went to hide in the walk-in fridge downstairs, only to find my brother, Chase, already there. He was bartending back then.

"What do we do?" he asked. Then: "It's soooo baaad."

"I don't know," I said. "But I'm staying down here until he leaves."

A few moments later, Elise, the waitress—who later became my partner—opened the fridge door. She didn't even blink when she saw us. "Wow. That guy is bad," she said, and sat down.

Despite it all, I stuck with brunch. Leaned into the poached eggs. Leaned into the whole thing. Eventually, we got so busy that I came up with this frittata to take some pressure off the flat-top (and me). I served it with salad, a rösti, sour cream, and pickled jalapeños on top. A definite hit.

CONTINUES

Preheat the oven to 375°F.

Heat a 10-inch cast-iron pan over medium heat. Add the olive oil, and then the mushrooms, onion, and kale. Cook for 10 minutes, adding more oil as needed and stirring occasionally so the onions don't burn and the kale cooks through. Season generously with salt and pepper. Pull it off the heat once the onions are just starting to go a little brown.

Crack the eggs into a large bowl. Add the cream and whisk thoroughly. (The better the whisk, the better the frittata will be. A flexible whisk does a better job than the cheap stiff ones.)

Pour the egg mixture straight into the pan, over the sautéed veg. Sprinkle the cheese over top and season with salt and pepper. Cover loosely with parchment paper.

Bake for 35 to 45 minutes, until the frittata is firm, with no jiggle in the middle. If there's a dip in the middle, she's not ready.

Serve with a dollop of sour cream and some pickled jalapeños on top.

Tomato Soup *with* Honey and Butter

SERVES 4

TOMATO SOUP

1 Tbsp olive oil

1 onion, roughly chopped

1 garlic clove, roughly chopped

Salt and ground black pepper

1 Tbsp tomato paste

3 cans (each 28 oz/796 mL) whole Roma tomatoes (the better the tomatoes, the better the soup)

½ tsp sugar

1 Tbsp butter

1 tsp honey

CHEESE TOASTIES

2 cups grated Cheddar, Swiss, or Gruyère cheese (or all three)

8 slices of your favorite bread (I use challah)

2 Tbsp duck fat or butter, for toasting

When I first opened for lunch at Union, I was thinking through a few solid options, and I kept coming back to this one. I remembered, as a kid, having Campbell's tomato soup with grilled cheese at my grandmother's house. So I leaned into the nostalgia and created this soup around that memory. It doesn't take very long. And it's a winner. A feel-good kind of soup.

MAKE THE SOUP: In a large pot over medium-high heat, heat the oil. Add the onion and garlic. Season with salt and pepper. Sauté for a few minutes, but don't let the onion brown—you want it soft, not caramelized. Stir in the tomato paste and cook, stirring, for 1 minute.

Pour in the tomatoes. Fill one of the empty cans with cold water and add that to the pot. Add the sugar to balance the acid and a pinch each of salt and pepper. Reduce the heat and simmer uncovered for 45 minutes, stirring occasionally.

Press the soup through a fine-mesh strainer with a ladle, breaking up the tomatoes to release the liquid. (The solids left behind make a great base for tomato sauce, so save them if you want.) Whisk the butter and honey into the strained soup.

Preheat the oven to 375°F. Line a baking sheet with parchment paper.

MAKE THE TOASTIES: Layer the grated cheese between the slices of bread to make four sandwiches.

In a large pan over medium heat, melt 1 Tbsp of the duck fat. Press two sandwiches into the fat to coat one side, then flip and press again so both sides get covered. Cook for about 2 minutes per side, keeping an eye on them so they don't burn, until the bread is golden and crisp on both sides. Transfer the sandwiches to the prepared baking sheet. Repeat with the remaining sandwiches, adding more duck fat as needed between batches.

CONTINUES

TABAC HACK

If you have leftover Béchamel Sauce (page 31), you can spread that and a little Dijon mustard on the bread before adding the cheese.

Place the sandwiches in the oven for a few minutes to finish, just until the cheese is hot and gooey.

Serve the bowls of soup with the toasties on the side.

Union Salad

SERVES 2 AS A MAIN, 4 AS AN APPETIZER

RÖSTI

3 potatoes (Yukon Golds or Russets; see Tabac Hack)

½ shallot, diced

Salt and ground black pepper

2 cups canola oil, for frying

UNION SALAD

4 slices thick-cut bacon

2 heads butter lettuce (or 1 head green leaf lettuce), separated into leaves

1 Tbsp olive oil (we use Alhema from Spain)

1 tsp grainy triple crunch mustard (I like Kozlik's)

¾ tsp red wine vinegar (we use a Pinot vinegar from Niagara)

1¾ oz (50 g) chèvre, at room temperature

Drizzle of honey

Cracked black pepper

This is one of five iconic dishes at Union. I made it on opening night, and it never left. I was trying to emulate an Au Petit Fer à Cheval salad—with the Bayonne ham and chèvre crostini—using the best ingredients I could find close to Union. It's all about how the rösti, chèvre, bacon, and honey come together with fresh organic lettuce and the à la minute vinaigrette of olive oil, triple crunch mustard, and Pinot (red wine) vinegar.

MAKE THE RÖSTI: Bring a pot of water to a boil, then add the whole potatoes. Boil for 5 minutes, then take the pot off the heat and let the potatoes sit in the hot water until they're cool enough to handle. Peel and grate them. You get a good deal of starch this way, which helps the rösti hold together and fry up real nice.

In a large bowl, combine the grated potato, shallot, and a pinch each of salt and pepper. Wet your hands to keep the mixture from sticking, then shape the potato mixture into four little cylinders.

In a medium saucepan, heat the canola oil to 375°F. Gently drop the rösti in and fry until golden brown, about 4 to 5 minutes. (If they float, you may need to turn them.)

Fry the bacon the way you like it. Some prefer crispy; others like it less so. Set aside.

Making a great salad is an art, so respect the moment. Place the lettuce leaves in a large bowl and tear them in half. Add the olive oil, mustard, and red wine vinegar. Season with salt and pepper. Give it a good toss with tongs. I morph into an old French guy, giving the salad some force as well as a gentle lovingness. Taste it. If you find it too sharp, add a little more mustard and olive oil until you have a nice balance. If it's too wet, add a bit more lettuce.

CONTINUES

TABAC HACK

I use Russets in the late winter months, when potatoes have spent a long time in cellars. I find they have less sugar than Yukon Golds and won't burn as fast in the oil.

Divide the lettuce into two shallow bowls (or four bowls if serving as an appetizer), staying toward the middle and inside the rim. Place the rösti on top, then the bacon over that. Use two spoons to shape the chèvre into quenelles and set them gently on top. Drizzle a little honey over the chèvre and finish with cracked black pepper.

Château Rouge

STEAK AND TOMATO TARTINE

SERVES 2

- 1 top sirloin steak (7 oz/200 g) (see Tabac Hack)
- Tenderizing Steak Marinade (page 135)
- 2 ripe beefsteak tomatoes
- Salt and ground black pepper
- Pinch of sugar
- 1 demi-baguette, halved lengthwise
- Good-quality olive oil
- 1 garlic clove
- Malt Mayo (page 285)
- Fresh basil leaves

When I first arrived in Paris, the owners of SoMo—the restaurant that hired us—put Chris and me up in an apartment in the 18th arrondissement, near the Château Rouge Métro station. It was a thrilling mash-up of chaos—people, markets, street vendors, and a live chicken shop a few doors down. The restaurant was in the 2nd arrondissement. After service, we'd usually hit a bar around the corner, then finish off at the Lowrider, which was open all night, or head to the Tambour to eat steak frites or a braised lamb shank at two in the morning. The Métro would be long closed by then, so we'd hike an hour and a half up the hill, past the Moulin Rouge and places I'd only seen in movies, dodging muggers along the way and making it home frozen, exhausted, and relieved.

I came up with this dish at Union when we started opening for lunch. I called it the Château Rouge as an ode to that raw Paris time when everything felt thrilling, jumbled, helpless, and alive, all in the same day and night.

Place the steak in a bowl. Pour the marinade over the steak, making sure it is fully coated. Cover and refrigerate for at least 3 hours, or overnight if possible.

Bring a large pot of water to a boil and set up an ice bath nearby. Using a small knife, gently score an X on the bottom of each tomato. Blanch the tomatoes for 10 to 15 seconds, then transfer them to the ice bath. After about a minute, peel off the skins, slice the tomatoes, and lay them out on a plate. Season with salt, pepper, and sugar. Let them sit for at least 30 minutes.

Preheat a grill or cast-iron pan (it's kind of awesome on a grill). Sear the steak for about 5 minutes per side for medium-rare. Let it rest for 15 minutes, then quickly sear again for about 1 minute per side to reheat. Slice the steak thinly against the grain.

CONTINUES

TABAC HACKS

Top sirloin is an affordable, flavorful cut from the top of the sirloin. It's a little tougher than pricier steaks, but the tenderizing marinade works magic here.

If you have any Galangal Glaze (page 287) lying around, drizzle that over the tartine as well.

Toast the baguette halves until golden. Drizzle with olive oil and rub with the garlic.

To assemble, smear malt mayo on the baguette halves, then layer on the tomatoes and steak. Season lightly with salt and pepper. Top with basil and a drizzle of olive oil.

Steak Tartare *with* Duck Fat Toast

SERVES 1

5 oz (150 g) medium ground eye of round steak (see Tabac Hack)

1 Tbsp lemony olive oil (we use Alhema from Spain)

1 tsp Dijon mustard

1 tsp soy sauce

Salt and ground black pepper

1 Tbsp duck fat

3 slices cornbread (½ inch thick)

Bread-and-Butter Pickles (page 280)

Habanero Sauce (page 288)

Dijon mustard

Grainy triple crunch mustard (I like Kozlik's)

TABAC HACK

Get your butcher to grind the eye of round fresh for you—ideally the day you serve it.

There was a time in Paris when everything I cooked felt off, inauthentic. But then I got an opportunity to cook at a small hotel in Alba, Italy. The night I arrived, Nico, the owner, picked me up from the airport, and we stopped at his father's tavern in Torino. Everything his dad dished out that night thrilled me; I wasn't expecting that kind of food in Italy. It reminded me of my grandparents' cooking and sparked a belief in me that I actually had cooking roots I could grow from. One of the courses was a veal tartare that was vibrant and light, with lemon, olive oil, and sea salt. When I returned home and opened Union, I couldn't stop thinking about it. I made my own version, the way I imagined it would taste at my grandparents' table.

I built the tartare around a citrusy Spanish olive oil for body, Dijon for some kick, and soy sauce for depth, with salt, pepper, and my grandmother's bread-and-butter pickles on top. We served it on hot duck fat toast—usually cornbread from a Portuguese bakery up the street back then. When we first opened, a loud TV chef who happened to be eating it at the bar yelled, "This needs hot sauce!" He wasn't wrong, so we serve it with a little homemade habanero sauce (something my friend Mike made one day). Now it's a staple on the dish and at the restaurant.

In a small bowl, mix the steak, olive oil, mustard, and soy sauce. Season with salt and pepper to taste. Mix again. If it's too bland, add a touch more mustard. If it's too strong, add a little more meat and a drizzle of olive oil to tone it down. If it's lacking depth, add a little more soy sauce.

In a medium pan over medium heat, heat the duck fat. Sear the cornbread on both sides until golden.

Pack the tartare into a ring mold or small ramekin and turn it out onto a plate. Arrange the toast around it, then top the tartare with the pickles and a small dollop each of the habanero sauce, Dijon mustard, and triple crunch mustard.

Elk Sliders

MAKES 16 SLIDERS

- 1 lb (450 g) ground elk (or venison or bison)
- ½ lb (225 g) ground beef
- 1 Tbsp smooth Dijon mustard
- 1 Tbsp soy sauce
- 1 tsp pure maple syrup
- Pinch each of salt and ground black pepper
- 3 Tbsp duck fat, divided
- 4 slices challah or any thick, soft bread
- 4 heaping tsp Spicy Mayo (page 286)
- ¼ cup Galangal Glaze (page 287)
- Bread-and-Butter Pickles (page 280)

TABAC HACK

This is a good opportunity to build up your pantry. The spicy mayo, pickles, and galangal glaze all last a long time in the fridge, and they're my go-tos for catering, along with Pickled Jalapeños (page 282), Hotel Butter (page 283), and Aioli (page 285).

Right before Union opened, I had a bunch of farmers over at my father's farm and threw a Paris-style dinner. I cooked everything on the wood-burning stove in the kitchen, right next to the old wood-planked sewing table where everyone sat. There was an apple farmer, a beef farmer, an elk farmer, a pheasant farmer, and a woman who was the town doctor—she raised Appleyard ducks too. It was an exciting time, and a hell of a night. One of the farmers, David, had just started the 100 Mile Market in town. He raised elk too. Meeting him that night gave me the idea for these sliders. We served them at Union on opening night, and they've never left the menu.

In a medium bowl, using your hands, mix the elk and beef with the mustard, soy sauce, maple syrup, salt, and pepper until it comes together.

Shape into thick silver dollar–sized patties, about 1¾ oz (50 g) each. You want them tall enough to stay medium-rare inside. You should get about 16 sliders. Put them on a plate and hit them with a little more salt and pepper before they hit the pan.

In a large pan over medium heat, warm the 1 Tbsp duck fat. Sear the sliders in two batches, pressing them down slightly to get a nice golden crust, for about 1½ minutes per side, depending on thickness. Add another 1 Tbsp duck fat between batches if needed. Transfer the sliders to a plate and let them rest while you toast the bread.

In a separate pan, warm the remaining 1 Tbsp duck fat. Working in batches if needed, toast the bread until golden on each side. (Or toast the bread in a toaster and spread some duck fat onto each piece.)

Smear 1 heaping tsp of spicy mayo on each piece of toast and cut it into four pieces. Top each piece with a slider, drizzle with the glaze, and finish with a couple of pickles.

Ra

Union Burger

SERVES 4

1½ lb (700 g) fatty ground beef (see Tabac Hack)
1 Tbsp Dijon mustard
1 Tbsp soy sauce
1 tsp pure maple syrup
1 tsp salt, divided
1 tsp ground black pepper, divided
1 Tbsp duck fat
4 slices Swiss cheese (or Cheddar)
4 slices bacon
4 soft brioche buns
Spicy Mayo (page 286)
Butter lettuce (or green leaf lettuce)
Galangal Glaze (page 287)
Bread-and-Butter Pickles (page 280)
Habanero Sauce (page 288)

TABAC HACK

Get your ground beef from your local butcher, who will probably use a mix of rib cap and chuck. It'll make for more flavorful burgers than buying a package of lean ground beef from the grocery store.

The burger at Union came together organically. I came up with the mix in Paris, brainstorming with a friend who wanted to open a burger spot. He wanted a juicy medium-rare burger, and the Dijon–soy–maple trio gave it the depth and balance for the beef to shine. The spicy mayo came from cooking in Chinatown with Chris on Sunday nights. When Union opened, I found some awesome smoky bacon from a German guy near the farm who had a beautiful old-school smoker he'd use on weekends because the new mechanical one he had to buy didn't have the same subtle smoke. Since I was already getting a mild Swiss cheese for the Swiss Train Ride, I put that on the burger too and finished it with a touch of galangal glaze.

In a large bowl, mix the beef, mustard, soy sauce, maple syrup, ½ tsp salt, and ½ tsp pepper. Shape into four patties about 2 inches thick. (When you cook them, you're aiming for a red, juicy center.) Season again with salt and pepper.

Heat a large pan over medium heat (not too hot, or the maple syrup will burn) with your duck fat. Season the patties with the remaining ½ tsp each salt and pepper. Cook the patties for 6 minutes, then flip. Top with cheese right after the flip so it melts while the patties finish cooking, another 6 minutes or so. Once the patties are done, let them rest in the pan off the heat. (If I'm in a pinch and buy ground beef from a grocery store, I'll cook my burgers to medium-well, but if I have my beef ground at a butcher shop and use it the same day, I'll cook them to medium-rare.)

While the burgers are resting, fry the bacon and toast the buns.

Cut the buns open and spread spicy mayo on both sides. Lay the patties on the bottom halves and lettuce on the top halves. Place one slice of bacon on each burger, then drizzle with galangal glaze. Top with pickles. Close up the burgers. Serve with a little habanero sauce on the side.

Polenta Gratin

SERVES 6

POLENTA

1 Tbsp olive oil

1 onion, finely diced

3 garlic cloves, grated

7 cups water

1 cup whole milk

2 cups instant polenta

7 oz (200 g) Piave cheese, grated

1 tsp salt

Chili flakes

5 cups canola oil, for frying

TOMATO SAUCE

Olive oil

1 onion, diced

2 garlic cloves, grated

1 can (14 oz/398 mL) good-quality whole Roma tomatoes, crushed with your hands

3 cups tomato passata

1 tsp salt

½ tsp sugar

BRAISED GREENS

Leafy greens (kale or Swiss chard work best)

Extra virgin olive oil

Salt and ground black pepper

TO FINISH

2 slabs Taleggio cheese (1¾ oz/50 g total)

Grated Piave cheese

Chili Jam (page 288)

This might be the best vegetarian dish I've ever made. It hits all the soft spots—it's crispy, lush, and melty. I put it on Union's menu when we opened, and it's never come off. Tambour and Heart's now do their own versions. Make the polenta and tomato sauce the day before if you can; it makes the dish even better. But if you're cooking them the morning of, that works too.

Line a glass lasagna dish with plastic wrap.

MAKE THE POLENTA: In a heavy-bottomed pot, heat the olive oil over medium heat. Add the onion and garlic, and sauté for about 5 minutes, until the onion is soft and translucent, not browned. Add the water and milk and bring to a boil. Slowly whisk in the polenta, whisking constantly to prevent clumps. You want it smooth and cooked thoroughly. As it starts to thicken, stir in the Piave, salt, and a few chili flakes. Watch the texture here. You want it thick, so it deep-fries properly. If it's too soft, it will break apart when you fry it. If needed, add a bit of milk or water to loosen it.

Once the polenta has had its bubble-and-spit moment, give it one last good whisk and pour it into the lined dish. It should flow out with a little help from a spatula. Smooth the top, press a piece of parchment paper right onto the surface, and chill in the fridge for at least 4 hours or overnight to set.

MAKE THE TOMATO SAUCE: Meanwhile, in a big, shallow pan over medium heat, pour in a generous glug of olive oil (this is one of those Italian nonna secrets you just have to trust). Add the onion and sauté for 1 minute, then add the garlic and sauté for 4 to 5 minutes, until everything's soft, translucent, and fragrant.

CONTINUES

TABAC HACKS

When I cooked this dish in Paris, I used Morbier cheese, a soft-rind cheese like Taleggio.

While your tomato sauce simmers, if you're feeling ambitious, roast some carrots or parsnips to serve on the side. Peel and chop, and toss with olive oil, salt, and pepper. Place on a baking sheet, cover with foil, and roast at 400°F for 45 minutes, until soft and flavorful.

Add the tomatoes and passata, then stir in the salt and sugar. Partially cover with a lid or place some parchment paper loosely over top so steam can escape. Simmer on low heat for 2 hours, stirring occasionally so it doesn't burn. For the last 30 minutes, take off the lid (or parchment) and let the sauce reduce.

Once the polenta is fully set, cut it into 3-inch squares. You should get at least six to eight pieces, depending on the size of your lasagna dish.

FRY THE POLENTA: In a medium pot, heat the canola oil to 375°F. Fry the polenta in batches of two at a time, turning to ensure equal cooking. They'll take about 7 minutes to get crisp and golden. If they're browning too fast, the oil's too hot (just turn the heat down a bit). Transfer the fried polenta to a plate.

BRAISE THE GREENS: Add 2 inches of water to a small pot and bring to a boil. Add the greens and cook for 2 minutes, until tender. Drain and dress with the olive oil, salt, and pepper.

Preheat the oven to 425°F.

TO ASSEMBLE: Spoon the tomato sauce into a 9 × 13-inch deep oven-safe dish, generously covering the bottom. Nestle the greens in the center and lay the fried polenta on top. Lay the Taleggio over the polenta, then grate some extra Piave around the dish.

Bake for 15 minutes, until the tomato sauce is bubbling and the cheese is gooey. Portion out on individual plates and top each with a hit of chili jam.

Fried Chicken Sandwich

MAKES 6 SANDWICHES

2 lb (900 g) boneless, skinless chicken thighs

1 batch Chicken, Hen or Rabbit Brine (page 284)

⅔ cup buttermilk

½ bunch fresh rosemary, stemmed and chopped

⅓ cup packed brown sugar

Canola or vegetable oil, for frying

DREDGE MIX

1½ cups all-purpose flour

⅔ cup potato starch

1½ Tbsp salt

1½ Tbsp ground white pepper

1½ Tbsp ground black pepper

1½ Tbsp paprika

1½ Tbsp dried thyme

1½ Tbsp onion powder

1½ Tbsp garlic powder

1½ Tbsp ground cumin

1½ Tbsp ground coriander

1½ Tbsp dried sage

1½ Tbsp Korean ground red pepper (gochugaru)

FOR SERVING

6 buns

Spicy Mayo (page 286)

Lettuce

Bread-and-Butter Pickles (page 280) or Pickled Jalapeños (page 282)

Everyday Slaw (page 255, optional)

We get a solid lunch crowd at Union, which has allowed us to lock in some routines. One of them is fried chicken on Fridays. It's become a thing, rolling into Saturday's busy lunch rush. This one's Matt's recipe. He's been at Union for a long time and has perfected this fried chicken—it's crispy, a little herby, and super tender.

The day before you want to make the sandwiches, place the chicken thighs in a large bowl or container and pour the brine over them. Add the buttermilk, rosemary, and brown sugar, and mix to combine. Cover and refrigerate overnight.

MAKE THE DREDGE MIX: In a large bowl, combine the flour and potato starch, then mix in the salt, white pepper, black pepper, paprika, thyme, onion powder, garlic powder, cumin, coriander, sage, and Korean pepper. Stir until evenly blended.

Divide the dredge mix equally into two bowls and set one aside. Remove the chicken from the marinade, discarding the marinade. One piece at a time, coat the chicken in dredge mix, pressing the coating firmly onto the surface. Cover the coated chicken and refrigerate for 30 to 60 minutes (or longer, if needed, while you're getting the rest of your meal together).

When ready to cook, use the second half of the dredge mix to coat the chicken again, one piece at a time. (This second dredge is just to clean up any loose patches—the first coating will still be damp enough for it to stick.)

Fill a deep, heavy-bottomed pot or a deep fryer halfway with canola oil and heat to 325°F.

Carefully lower the chicken into the hot oil. Fry for about 8 minutes, until the chicken is crisp and a deep golden brown, and has reached an internal temperature of at least 165°F. Using a fryer basket, slotted spoon, or tongs, transfer the chicken to a wire rack or paper towel to drain excess oil.

CONTINUES

TABAC HACK

Instead of the sage and thyme, you can use 3 Tbsp of dried herbes de Provence.

TO SERVE: Toast the buns and spread with spicy mayo. Add lettuce, the fried chicken, and either pickles or jalapeños. Top with slaw, if desired. Let the chicken do the work and keep the rest pretty simple.

2%
Keep
refrigerated
1 LITRE

Arctic Char *with* Sweet Mustard Sauce and Dressed Beets

SERVES 4

SWEET MUSTARD SAUCE

1 large egg yolk

1 Tbsp Dijon mustard

1 tsp sugar

1 tsp Pernod liqueur

Squeeze of lemon juice

1 cup canola oil

Salt

4 beets

1 Tbsp olive oil (a dressing olive oil)

Kosher salt and ground black pepper

4 pieces (5 oz/150 g each) arctic char (nice middle sections)

1 tsp duck fat or preferred cooking oil

Squeeze of lemon juice

Rösti (page 105), for serving (optional)

When Union was young, there was real energy in the restaurant scene—small, independent places doing ambitious things on shoestring budgets. I kept my head down, caught somewhere between survival mode and mourning my father, though I didn't realize it at the time. But looking back through the food in this book, I see the influence of those small places. They were doing exciting work. They inspired me. They pushed me to do better. In hindsight, it feels like luck that I made it through, because a lot of those places didn't. Restaurants are notoriously tough to run. You've got 3 years to get through the muck and heartache. If your place hasn't been torn to shreds and burned up in the atmosphere of ambition—by the city, the repair bills, the weather, the taxes—then maybe you've got a shot at building something special. But those 3 years are rough. And if you knew how rough, you probably wouldn't do it. These days, rents are higher, the costs of building a place are up, and it feels like there's less space for those smaller, heartfelt, dreamer places that once gave the city its pulse.

I first made a version of this dish at Union, back when we were one of the only spots serving lunch. The sweet mustard, earthy beets, and fish just *worked*—and the room was always full of chefs and industry folks, the kind of eclectic crowd that kept me on my toes. It was a crowd-pleaser then, and it still is.

MAKE THE SAUCE: Add the egg yolk, mustard, sugar, Pernod, and lemon juice to a blender. Blend to combine. With the motor running, slowly add the canola oil, letting the sauce emulsify and turn creamy. Season with a touch of salt to taste. Set aside.

CONTINUES

TABAC HACK

You can use rainbow trout instead of the arctic char and cook it the same way.

Bring a pot of salted water to a boil. Add the beets and cook until tender, about 45 minutes. Remove from the water, trim the ends, and rub off the skins with a paper towel. Cut into quarters and dress with a little olive oil, salt, and pepper.

Season both sides of the arctic char generously with salt and pepper. In a nonstick pan over medium heat, heat the duck fat. Add the char, skin side down, and cook for 6 minutes (no need to flip). Watch the flesh cook itself through. If you want to cook it well (or it's a stubborn or fatty piece), give it a flip at the last moment and sear for another 30 seconds.

Spoon a generous smear of the sweet mustard sauce onto each plate. Place the dressed beets on the sauce and place the char on top, skin side down. Finish with a squeeze of lemon over the fish. Serve with the rösti alongside, if desired.

Halibut *with* Shrimp Butter Sauce and Fried Capers

SERVES 4

FRIED CAPERS

Neutral oil (canola, sunflower, or grapeseed)

Handful of capers, drained

Salt

SHRIMP BUTTER SAUCE

½ lb (225 g) butter

6 wild-caught shrimp, peeled and deveined (save the shells and tails)

Salt

HALIBUT

Olive oil

4 halibut fillets (about 5 oz/150 g each)

Salt and ground black pepper

Lemon wedges, for serving

A chef named Dan gave me a job when I first got back to Toronto. Eventually, I was able to return the favor when he did a stint running the line at Union. He was a big, kind, loving cook. He passed way too young, and I wanted to honor him with this dish. I learned this move from him on the line at Union. He poached shrimp in butter, giving it a reddish hue and seafood depth. It's everything you imagine melted butter with shellfish should be.

MAKE THE FRIED CAPERS: In a small pan over medium heat, heat about 1 inch of oil to 375°F. Carefully add the capers—they'll pop and open like little flowers. Fry for about 1 minute, until crispy and light golden brown. Remove with a slotted spoon, transfer to a paper towel, and season with salt.

MAKE THE SAUCE: In a small saucepan over medium-low heat, melt the butter. Add the shrimp tails and shells. Let the butter poach and foam a little, but you don't want it to brown or separate, just to be enriched with flavor. Strain out the shells and return the butter to the pot.

Chop the shrimp into small pieces and add them to the butter. Poach over medium heat for 1 to 2 minutes, until the shrimp are firm, pink, and opaque. The butter should foam but not split. Season with salt to taste and set aside.

COOK THE HALIBUT: Heat a large cast-iron or nonstick pan over medium heat. Add a drizzle of olive oil and listen for a lively sizzle. Season the halibut generously on both sides with salt and pepper (I do this on a plate so I can press and pick up the loose seasoning). Place the fillets flesh side down in the pan and sear for about 5 minutes, until golden. Flip and cook for another 3 to 4 minutes, until the fish is opaque and flakes easily with a fork. Remove from the heat.

CONTINUES

Bring the shrimp sauce to a boil for a moment, so it's hot and lively.

Plate the halibut and spoon the sauce over top, making sure there are some shrimp on top of the fish and the rest spill over the sides. Top with the fried capers and finish with a squeeze of lemon.

Roast Hen *with* Chalet Sauce

SERVES 4

HENS

2 hens (1½ lb/700 g each)

1 Tbsp Rib Rub (page 131)

1 Tbsp Cure Mix (page 183)

BLANCHED GREENS

1 bunch Swiss chard, stems cut separate from the leaves

Olive oil, for drizzling

CHALET SAUCE

⅓ cup chicken stock

⅓ cup Rib Sauce (page 131)

½ tsp Galangal Glaze (page 287)

1 Tbsp Hotel Butter (page 283)

One of the stops my cousin and I made before going to Morocco was in Switzerland, to visit our grandparents in Saanenmöser. They were well into their 70s and still skiing. We had dinner at the chalet hotel and were served roast chicken with a sauce that I immediately recognized as *real* Swiss chalet sauce. I've been chasing it ever since. Maybe it was the comfort of being with our grandparents, eating warm food in a hotel after backpacking our way there.

MARINATE THE HENS: Cut the hens in half and rub them all over with the rib rub and cure mix. Place them in an airtight container and let them marinate in the fridge for up to 4 hours.

Preheat the oven to 400°F.

ROAST THE HENS: Place the hens in a roasting pan and roast for 55 minutes. Check if they need more time. They should smell amazing and look reddish-golden, glistening, and sizzling—not loud, greasy, or smoky, but a calm, happy sizzle. If they're not making any noise or don't have juices pooling in the pan, give them another 10 minutes or so. The internal temperature should be 165°F.

BLANCH THE GREENS: While the hens are roasting, bring 1 cup of salted water to a boil in a medium pot. Add the chard—stems first, leaves on top—so the stems boil while the leaves steam. Blanch for 3 minutes, then use tongs to stir the leaves into the water to make sure they're cooked through. Cook for another 30 seconds. Drain any remaining water, toss with the olive oil, cover, and set aside.

Transfer the roasted hens to a plate to rest uncovered.

CONTINUES

TABAC HACKS

When you're preparing a sauce, focus on it; don't have other pots boiling or things pulling your attention away. Just be with the sauce. It'll make the whole meal better, and you'll actually feel settled when you sit down to eat.

If you want more zing, hit the chalet sauce with a couple of dashes of Frank's RedHot sauce to give it that extra je ne sais quoi.

MAKE THE SAUCE: As soon as the hens come out, set the roasting pan over medium heat and deglaze with the chicken stock. It should start to simmer and reduce right away. Let it reduce by half. Whisk the rib sauce, galangal glaze, and hotel butter into the simmering sauce. Pour in any juices that have collected under the hens while they've been resting, then bring the sauce back up to piping hot.

Divide the greens among four plates. Carve the hens and set the pieces on top. Pour the chalet sauce over and serve the rest alongside in a gravy boat.

Sticky Ribs

SERVES 4 TO 6

RIB SAUCE (see Tabac Hack)

2 cups canned whole tomatoes

1 cup packed brown sugar

1 cup white vinegar

½ cup soy sauce

1 onion, diced

2 garlic cloves, smashed

1 Tbsp Pickled Jalapeños (page 282)

RIB RUB

3 Tbsp paprika

1 Tbsp curry powder

1 Tbsp salt

1 Tbsp ground black pepper

RIBS

4 racks pork back ribs (about 5 to 6 lb/2.3 to 2.7 kg total)

2 Tbsp canola oil or duck fat, for searing

TABAC HACK

Pour off about 1 cup of the rib sauce and set it aside for the Barbecued Habanero Wings (page 269) and/or the Chalet Sauce (page 129).

There was a little takeout rib spot called Mickey's Ribs around the corner from my house when I was growing up. My dad would bring ribs home on special occasions, and we'd eat them on his bed and watch TV. The sauce was both sweet and sour, and the ribs were tender and smoky. These ribs, inspired by those memories, have been a staple at Union since the beginning.

Preheat the oven to 450°F. Pull out the bottom rack so you can place the pan directly on the bottom of the oven.

MAKE THE SAUCE: In a large bowl, combine the tomatoes, brown sugar, vinegar, soy sauce, onion, garlic, and jalapeños. Squeeze the tomatoes with your hands to break them up. Whisk together, ensuring the brown sugar is evenly incorporated (it's going to want to settle on the bottom, and you don't want to lose out on any of it).

MAKE THE RUB: In a small bowl, mix the paprika, curry powder, salt, and pepper.

PREP THE RIBS: Rub the spice mixture all over the ribs, front and back. If the racks won't fit in your pan, cut them in half.

SEAR THE RIBS: In a large pan over medium heat, heat the oil. Working in batches, sear the ribs for 3 to 4 minutes per side, until browned. Add more oil between batches as needed.

BRAISE AND ROAST THE RIBS: Lay the ribs flesh side down in a large, heavy-bottomed roasting pan. If needed, lean them on each other to fit—meatier sides on the bottom. Pour the sauce over top. Cover tightly with foil.

CONTINUES

Place the pan directly on the bottom of the oven. (This is so the ribs braise and roast, and the sauce reduces to a glaze.) Cook for about 1 hour. You should smell them by then. If the meat pulls from the bone, they are cooked just enough. If it's pulling off too much, don't worry; they'll tighten back up on the barbecue. But try not to overcook them, or all the flavor and fat will end up in the sauce instead of the meat.

Lift the ribs out of the sauce and set them aside. Keep the sauce—you'll need it later. (You can roast the ribs a few hours ahead of time, let them cool in the sauce, cover and refrigerate them until you're ready to grill, and then barbecue them before dinner. They're easier to handle once they've cooled down.)

BARBECUE THE RIBS: Fire up a charcoal grill and get some coals going. When they're hot, push them to one side and place the ribs, flesh side up, on the cooler side, away from the coals. Cover with the lid, vents open, and grill for 45 to 60 minutes. You're looking for a reddish-caramel hue and a skin that's tight, almost crisp.

Heat the reserved sauce in a saucepan. If it's too loose, reduce it. Pour it over the hot-off-the-grill ribs. (If you barbecue the ribs earlier, you can heat them back up with the sauce for dinner—just like we do for service at the restaurant.)

Bavette Frites *with* Hotel Butter and Aioli

SERVES 4

TENDERIZING STEAK MARINADE

1 cup soy sauce (see Tabac Hack)

1 garlic clove, grated

1 Tbsp ground black pepper

½ tsp baking soda (see Tabac Hack)

¾ cup water

1¾ lb (800 g) flank steak

1 tsp duck fat or beef tallow

HOME FRITES

8 Yukon Gold or Russet potatoes (Russets are best in winter)

2 tsp salt, divided

1 tsp baking soda

4 cups canola oil

4 Tbsp beef tallow or duck fat (optional)

4 Tbsp Hotel Butter (page 283), for serving

½ cup Aioli (page 285), for serving

Before I moved to Paris, my friend Chris was renting a house with a few other guys in Toronto's Chinatown. On Sundays, we'd cook dinner together and invite everyone we knew—mostly students from the art school around the corner. I'd head down to Chinatown because it was the most affordable place to shop and pick up a big slab of bavette. We'd marinate it in soy sauce and beer with a spoonful of baking soda to tenderize it. When I opened Union, I reworked that old Chinatown marinade, using my grandfather's steak marinade as inspiration. It became the one we use for our steak frites.

TENDERIZE THE STEAK: In a large bowl, whisk together the soy sauce, garlic, pepper, and baking soda. It should bubble a bit to show that the baking soda's still active. Add the water and stir to combine.

Place the steak in the bowl and make sure it's immersed. Cover and refrigerate for 4 to 6 hours.

START THE FRITES: In the last hour of the steak marinating, prepare the potatoes by peeling them, trimming the ends, and cutting lengthwise into even fries—1 inch thick for big fries, or about ½ inch for thinner frites. Rinse in cold water, stirring with your hands, until the water runs clear, about a minute.

Fill a large pot about three-quarters full with water. Add 1 tsp salt and the baking soda. Parboil the fries until just tender (see Tabac Hack). Drain and spread them on a wire rack set over a sheet pan—or on parchment if you don't have one—and place in the freezer to cool for 30 minutes.

When the steak's almost ready to cook, heat the canola oil and tallow, if using, in a large pot to 285°F. Working in batches, blanch the fries for 3 minutes. Remove and spread them back on the tray, then freeze again for another 30 minutes.

CONTINUES

TABAC HACKS

Not all soy sauces are created equal. Some are just salt bombs with no depth. Yummy House is a great pick—affordable, balanced, and actually flavorful.

A small amount of baking soda helps break down the muscle fibers and tenderize the meat. And make sure to check the expiry date—baking soda can lose its power.

For extra-crispy fries, sprinkle the fries with a little potato starch after the first blanch and toss to coat before putting them in the freezer.

To check a steak's doneness, stick a knife into the middle and then touch your lip with it. If the knife is cool, the steak is blue. If the knife is cool-warm, the steak is rare. If the knife is warm, the steak is medium-rare. If the knife is hot, the steak is medium to well done.

COOK THE STEAK: Heat a heavy-bottomed skillet over medium heat and add the duck fat. When the pan's hot, add the steak—it should sizzle and start to tighten up when it hits the pan, but it shouldn't smoke. Now leave it alone. Cook for 7 to 10 minutes. Don't flip or nudge it around the pan. We're going for that deep golden sear. Flip and cook for another 5 to 7 minutes. You can use a knife to lip check it (see Tabac Hack). Set aside and rest.

FINISH THE FRITES: Bring the frying oil to 375°F and fry the fries until golden and crisp. Transfer to a stainless steel bowl lined with paper towel and toss with the remaining 1 tsp salt.

Divide the steaks and frites among four plates. Top each steak with a spoonful of hotel butter and serve the fries with a side of aioli.

Duck Confit with Orange Sauce

SERVES 4

DUCK CONFIT

4 duck legs (about 14 oz/400 g each)

4 garlic cloves, peeled and lightly smashed

A few sprigs fresh thyme

4 tsp salt

Freshly cracked black pepper

1 tsp honey

ORANGE SAUCE

1 cup freshly pressed orange juice

2 tsp orange marmalade

1 tsp soy sauce

1 Tbsp butter

My friend Chris has been around the cooking track a lot. And every time he refines what he does, little things fall away that he decides are no longer necessary. I've come to see the beauty and significance in that and admire him for it. He started cooking his duck confit in water instead of duck fat. The genius of it is that you end up with a nice little jus at the end, not a big tub of seasoned fat you have to store in the fridge until the next time you confit. The duck still comes out crispy and flavorful. I added a little orange sauce because I still like a bit of bling, and I haven't been around the track as many times as Chris to fully shake the need for it.

PREPARE THE DUCK: The day before cooking, trim any excess fat from around the edges of the duck legs. Gently score the skin, then cut the tendon at the tip of each ankle joint so the skin doesn't pull back as it cooks. If you like, render the trimmed fat in a small saucepan with 1 teaspoon of water over medium-low heat until melted. Strain and set aside.

Rub the duck legs evenly with the garlic, thyme, salt, and pepper. Cover and refrigerate for at least 12 hours to cure. This helps the duck retain its flavor when cooked in water.

Preheat the oven to 250°F.

When ready to cook, rinse the salt from the legs and place them in a roasting pan. You can leave the garlic and thyme with the duck, then add enough water to come halfway up the legs. Stir in the honey, cover tightly with foil, and roast for about 3½ hours. The duck is ready when a paring knife slides easily into the meat; if it still feels resistant, give it another 30 minutes.

Transfer the legs to a plate to rest. Strain the cooking liquid into a container and refrigerate for a couple of hours, until the fat hardens on top of the jus. Lift off the fat and reserve the jus.

CONTINUES

Increase the oven temperature to 385°F. Add 1 tablespoon of the rendered duck fat to the pan and then return the duck legs to the pan as well. Roast uncovered for 20 minutes. Halfway through, flip the legs over, skin side down, to crisp up the skin.

MAKE THE ORANGE SAUCE: Add the orange juice and marmalade to a small saucepan over medium heat and reduce by half. Stir in the reserved duck jus and soy sauce and let simmer for a moment.

When the duck comes out of the oven, remove the duck legs and pour off any excess fat. Deglaze the roasting pan with the sauce, then whisk in the butter to give it a glossy finish. Season with salt and pepper to taste.

Transfer the duck legs to a warm platter and spoon the sauce over top to serve.

Butter Tarts

MAKES 12 TARTS

BLITZ PUFF PASTRY

2 cups all-purpose flour
¾ cup + 1 Tbsp cold butter
1½ tsp salt
1 tsp honey
1 tsp fresh lemon juice
½ cup cold water

FILLING

1 cup packed brown sugar
½ cup maple syrup
¼ cup butter
¼ cup heavy (35%) cream
1 tsp pure vanilla extract
½ tsp salt
2 eggs, lightly beaten
½ cup toasted pecans (optional, see page 206 for toasting nuts)

My grandmother June—we called her Gran—would make these on the regular. They were always sitting on the counter by the phone that hung on the wall. Some had raisins, some had nuts, but most were plain. After my grandfather and I came back from a walk in the fields or fishing at a lake nearby, we'd make some tea and a fire and eat them in the living room. My grandparents' place was a life-affirming pit stop when I was young, and even as I got older; it helped ground me in love.

MAKE THE PASTRY: In a stand mixer fitted with the paddle attachment, combine the flour, butter, salt, and honey. Mix on low speed until the butter is evenly distributed but still in large chunks. Add the lemon juice and cold water. Mix just until a dough forms, but don't overmix—you still want fairly large chunks of butter in the dough.

Turn the dough out onto a floured surface, flatten it, wrap it in plastic wrap, and chill for 30 minutes.

On a lightly floured surface, shape the chilled dough into a rough rectangle. Roll it out evenly, pressing from the center outward, until it's about ½ inch thick. The surface should look smooth but slightly marbled with visible streaks of butter. Dust with flour as needed to prevent sticking, lifting and turning the dough occasionally to keep the shape even.

With the dough lengthwise, fold one short end in toward the center by about one-third. Fold the opposite short end over the first so it fully covers it (like folding a letter). Press lightly. The piece should be a thick, three-layer rectangle. Turn the dough 90 degrees. Roll it out evenly to about ½ inch thick. Repeat the fold—one short end into the center, then the other over top. Repeat this sequence once more, then wrap the dough in plastic wrap and refrigerate for 30 minutes.

After chilling, repeat the same rolling and folding process two more times, for a total of five folds. Wrap the dough again and refrigerate for another 30 minutes.

CONTINUES

Preheat the oven to 350°F.

On a floured surface, roll out the pastry and cut out 4-inch circles. Press each circle into the bottom and up the sides of one cup of a 12-cup muffin tin. Fill the tart shells with pie weights. Bake for 20 minutes. Remove the pie weights and let the shells cool slightly.

MAKE THE FILLING: While the pastry is baking, in a small saucepan over low heat, combine the brown sugar, syrup, and butter, stirring until the butter is melted and the mixture is combined. Stir in the cream; the mixture will begin to bubble. Remove from the heat and stir in the vanilla and salt. Let cool slightly (just enough that the eggs won't scramble when you add it). Whisk in the eggs until smooth. Stir in the pecans (if using).

Fill the tart shells about two-thirds full with the filling, then return to the oven and bake for 15 minutes, or until the pastry is golden.

Let cool completely on a rack, then remove the tarts from the tin. Serve at room temperature.

Sticky Ginger Cake

SERVES 8 TO 10

CAKE

- 2 cups all-purpose flour
- 1 Tbsp baking powder
- 1½ tsp baking soda
- 4 tsp ground ginger
- 1 tsp ground allspice
- 1 tsp salt
- 1 cup packed brown sugar
- 1 cup fancy molasses
- ¾ cup corn syrup
- ½ cup candied ginger, chopped
- ½ cup + 2 Tbsp (or 1 stick) butter
- 2 eggs
- 1 cup milk

SALTED CARAMEL

- 1 lb (450 g) butter
- 2 cups packed brown sugar
- ⅓ cup white sugar
- 2 cups heavy (35%) cream
- Pinch of salt

Vanilla ice cream, for serving

Ross is the OG of the New Zealand chefs that have blessed the restaurants. He came over from London 14 years ago and helped put Union on the map. He has an amazing cooking force and a vast knowledge of food. One major hit he brought was his sticky ginger cake. It works with whipped cream or vanilla ice cream, but make sure they're not too sweet. It can make the dessert overwhelmingly sweet—something I learned the hard way when we were making our own ice cream and a table ordered it. I remember one guest yelling out, "My teeth are melting!" and I was like, oh wow, I think the ice cream is too sweet. We adjusted it to balance out with the caramel sauce and be a vehicle for the cake. The rest is history.

Preheat the oven to 350°F. Grease and line a 9 × 13-inch baking dish.

MAKE THE CAKE: In a large bowl, whisk together the flour, baking powder, baking soda, ground ginger, allspice, and salt. Sift and set aside.

In a medium saucepan, combine the brown sugar, molasses, corn syrup, candied ginger, and butter. Bring to a boil and stir occasionally. Let cool to room temperature.

Pour the cooled wet ingredients into the dry ingredients and whisk vigorously until smooth.

In a separate bowl, beat the eggs with the milk. Whisk the egg mixture into the batter until fully incorporated.

Pour the batter into the prepared pan. Bake for 40 to 50 minutes, until a skewer inserted in the center comes out clean. Cool completely in the dish.

MAKE THE SALTED CARAMEL: In a medium saucepan over medium heat, melt the butter with the brown sugar and whisk until smooth and melted.

CONTINUES

TABAC HACK

At Union, we reheat the cake and caramel in the microwave so it's gooey and piping hot for serving.

In a large saucepan over medium heat, combine the white sugar and 1 Tbsp water, stirring until it looks like wet sand. As it starts to caramelize and turn a golden color, add the butter mixture and let it bubble. Take off the heat and whisk in the cream. Add the salt and whisk to combine.

Cut the cake into square pieces and pour ¼ cup salted caramel over each portion. Serve with ice cream alongside.

Raspberry Lemon Cake

SERVES 8 TO 10

GENOISE

1⅓ cups all-purpose flour

¼ cup cornstarch

7 eggs

1 cup sugar

⅛ cup melted butter

LEMON CURD

½ cup sugar

5 egg yolks

1 tsp lemon zest

½ cup fresh lemon juice

½ cup butter, softened, cubed

RASPBERRY FILLING

14 oz (400 g) fresh raspberries

¼ cup sugar

2 Tbsp fresh lemon juice

1 tsp pure vanilla extract

2 tsp cornstarch

WHITE CHOCOLATE CHANTILLY

2 gelatin leaves

2 cups white chocolate chips

3½ cups heavy (35%) cream

2 tsp pure vanilla extract

12 fresh raspberries

When I open a restaurant, I always imagine that space becoming part of the world. Like anyone could walk in, at any moment, from anywhere. I put a lot of faith in the magic of that. And if you hold on long enough, it all comes true.

My friend Mike, who used to work at Union and Côte de Bœuf, now runs a food bank. One day, a chef from Marseille walked in, and Mike sent him over to Union. Sharaff Lawal is a pastry chef, and we made a home for him. Since then, he's been making these incredible desserts that have greatly added to the magic of Union, something we always wished for. This is one of those desserts—people really love it.

I'm still waiting for Bob Dylan to walk in one day.

Preheat the oven to 350°F. Line a 9 × 13-inch cake pan with parchment paper.

MAKE THE GENOISE: Sift the flour and cornstarch together into a bowl.

In a separate large bowl, whip the eggs and sugar until creamy yellow, about 4 to 5 minutes. Fold in the flour mixture, then gently fold in the melted butter. Pour the batter into the prepared pan.

Bake for 18 to 20 minutes, until a toothpick comes out clean. Cool in the pan for 10 minutes and then on a rack until completely cool.

MAKE THE CURD: In a small saucepan, combine the sugar, egg yolks, lemon zest, and lemon juice. Mix with a spatula to combine. Cook for 10 to 15 minutes, until it thickens.

Strain over a fine-mesh sieve and let it cool for 10 minutes. Add the butter and incorporate it with an immersion blender. Cool completely, then refrigerate until needed.

CONTINUES

MAKE THE FILLING: In another saucepan over medium heat, combine the raspberries, sugar, lemon juice, and vanilla. Bring to a simmer and simmer gently until the berries soften. Stir in the cornstarch and cook just until thickened. Let cool.

MAKE THE CHANTILLY: Soak the gelatin in cold water for 3 minutes. Squeeze out the excess water and add the gelatin to a large bowl with the white chocolate.

In a medium saucepan, bring the cream and vanilla to a boil. Pour over the chocolate and gelatin and, using an immersion blender, blend until smooth. Let cool.

Once completely cool, use an electric mixer to whip the chantilly to medium peaks.

ASSEMBLE THE CAKE: Using a long serrated knife, split the genoise into three even layers. Place one layer on a 9-inch cake board or serving plate. Spread a thin layer of the lemon curd over top, then spread about ¼ inch of chantilly over the curd. Spoon and gently spread a layer of raspberry filling over the cream.

Repeat with the second layer of cake: spread the lemon curd, then the chantilly, and lastly the raspberry filling. Place the final layer of cake on top. Spread a thin layer of chantilly over the top and sides to seal in any crumbs, then refrigerate for 30 minutes.

Spread another ¼-inch layer of chantilly evenly over the top and sides of the cake and refrigerate for 1 hour.

To finish, spoon a layer of lemon curd over the top, leaving a ½-inch border around the edge. Pipe more of the chantilly cream around the curd. Keep refrigerated until ready to serve.

CÔTE DE BŒUF
CÔTE DE BŒUF
BAR À VIN
Caviste
Hot n Cold
Sandwiches to go
Take out Menu

Côte de Bœuf

Côte de Bœuf

At Union, I was bringing in huge slabs of meat every Saturday from a farmer friend named Frank. His meat was incredible. It aged beautifully and had wonderful flavor, and once I discovered it, I pretty much built the menu at Union around it. The flavor reminded me of my grandmother's description of how meat used to taste—clean, without hormones. We'd dry-age the beef, hanging it next to the saucisson so that the white, dusty mold covering the sausage would influence the beef, helping it break down and age gracefully. The big slabs hanging in the Union basement looked beautifully stoic, like the meat I had seen hanging at Rungis Market. The skill of Frank's animal husbandry was developed over a generation of practice, passed down from his father to him. The feed was a special family mix, developed with the spirit of his father's character and instinct for cattle. The cattle grazed on vast, lush, bright green pastures most of the year. The barn in which they lived in the winter smelled of fermented grains and fresh hay.

We were doing the butchery of all the meat in the basement at Union with a handsaw, and it was becoming unmanageable. I had my friend Mike cracking the meat and trim and breaking it down on Mondays, but we'd run out by the weekend. It was a mad hustle. Sometimes I'd be hacking at a rib cut with a saw and grabbing a côte de bœuf and racing back upstairs to get it on the flat-top. It was pure theater on a whim. One time, an antique dealer named Mark brought down a huge, beautiful Amish-raised pig in the back of his beat-up pickup truck. It had been fed whey and vegetable scraps and had 3 inches of back fat. It was stiff and frozen from the winter drive into the city, and it took three of us to lug it downstairs. When we finally got it down there, Mike the butcher, seeing it stiff-legged and hanging half off the counter, had an incredible meltdown. It can take that level of misadventure for me to see what needs to be done. We needed more space.

By this time, I had paid myself back and stored up a little financial buffer for Union. My brother, Chasen, was living down the street, above a small flower shop filled with antiques. In the 1930s, the space had been a grocery store called Select Grocer, and then Kay's Convenience until the 90s—they sold chips, pop, and cigarettes with lots of cats hanging around. The next owners were hoping to rent it out, and my brother suggested we open a butcher shop. I could see the meat hanging in there, beef and pork butt and ducks and rabbits, like the old Paris butcher shops. I could imagine offering homemade terrines and rillettes, and serving French baguette sandwiches like they had at Au Petit Fer à Cheval—ham, Swiss, rosette de Lyon, and cornichon. So we signed a lease. It was a chance to see if I could build something all on my own, and I had a really good bookkeeper, Barry, to keep the books straight.

I knew the name immediately—Côte de Bœuf—so I had that going for me. But since my father wasn't with me this time around, I had to forage on my own for antiques to pull the place together and give it that Union feel, but more French-French. Those dusty, cold antique shops felt so lonely, and my heart sank as I stumbled around looking for stuff, with no one to bounce ideas off. I avoided a few places we used to go, not wanting to explain why he wasn't with me. Three years after his death, I was still full of sorrow, operating in a state of denial and disbelief. Hunting for the materials to build out a new place was another reminder that he was no longer here.

But I had some help. The owner, Stefano, was a carpenter and antique collector, and he had an endless stash of reclaimed wood in his shop in the back. He would go to Buffalo to shop at the big antique places around town, and he found many treasures, including a set of giant frosted-glass doors from the 1950s. I hired him to build the space. Since it was his building, he knew the ins and outs, and he had a great instinct for the finishing touches.

So while Union was a tough birth with many complications, Côte de Bœuf came together quickly and smoothly. There was no liquor license to apply for (I was going to do that later), so I didn't have to tangle with the city. I got my operating license under "food stuff," like a glorified convenience store. I figured if I disclosed my full plan and vision for the place, the city would never let it happen.

On opening night, there were côtes de bœuf and whole lambs hanging in the window. There were rabbits, and applewood-smoked chickens that I'd smoked at the farm and finished on the barbecue. They had come out plump and juicy, with a red hue, looking like Peking ducks. The place looked and felt and smelled like an old butcher shop from the early 20th century.

In the shop, there was a row of cupboards with iron-stenciled glass doors that I insulated and refrigerated. All the French cheese, charcuterie, heritage eggs, and terrines went in there, like an antique grab-and-go. Barbara Klunder, who had done the mural at Union, came back and painted a big bull on the floor and a little pig in the window above the front door. We put in French bistro–style white bullnose tile with black trim in the back, framing an old butcher's table like a cathedral. I found an art deco mirror from a train and put it in the corner, and added an antique corner hand sink underneath. We put an awning outside, and a local artist painted Côte de Bœuf on the window. Another friend made a stained-glass design of a Bellmora hat to honor my dad, who often wore one near the end of his life. It went above the bathroom, with a light behind it so it would glow at night. I put in a Garland flat-top with four burners and two ovens, and nestled a deep fryer next to it. We built a walk-in in the backyard, between the lilac trees. The place was a work of art, and I hoped it would be an atelier for artisans to buy good products and a place where they could refine their methods.

FOOD
STORE
SAGE

Frank would bring the meat in every Saturday morning, along with double-smoked bacon from a German spot up near his farm. Soon the walk-in was packed with hips, loins, and primes. We were making rillettes, terrines, sausages, and corned beef. Roast beef and truffle aioli sandwiches with Comté, rosette, butter, and cornichons became a staple. In the window were wheels of Brie de Meaux, yellow heritage chickens, and Mennonite eggs in green and brown shells.

But in those first months, the place struggled. Retail margins were razor-thin. You never had the product people wanted when they wanted it, and when you did, nobody wanted it. Labor costs stayed restaurant-level high. It was a brutal mix—a string of gut punches and quiet panic. My friend Chris, with whom I'd reconciled, started working at the shop. He'd lost the restaurant he'd opened in Paris and had come back to regroup. We were both tired, both lost, and cooking dinners together again—with nothing to prove anymore—was healing for us both.

So, we went into phase two: private dinners in the front room, applying for temporary liquor licenses once or twice a week. We set up a big oak art table that could seat 18. Chris led the dinners and I played wingman. His style was eclectic and simple—Marco Pierre White with a twist. We served scrambled duck eggs, slow-cooked, with applewood-smoked salmon folded in at the end; rabbit dumplings with rabbit bacon, carrot pancake, and jus; and côte de bœuf, family-style, with pommes sautées, just like at Robert et Louise in Paris. They were incredible dinners, but not sustainable. We needed the place humming every day by running Côte de Bœuf like a restaurant. Nothing beats butts in seats.

There's a place in Paris called the Baron Rouge, a throwback to a Hemingway-esque artists' hangout. On weekends, you could get 24 shucked oysters out front, then go inside and buy a bottle of Muscadet or Sancerre or Pinot Noir from Bourgogne, or all three if you were feeling dangerous. The place was jammed and loud and rambunctious with music. It had a zinc-topped bar with bistro lights over top. You could fill up a jug from barrels of wholesale wine on your way home.

The empty barrels were scattered around and used as tables. You'd come out with the wine, oysters, and charcuterie, and use the hoods of cars as tables. It was an amazing way to spend a weekend afternoon in Paris. I wanted Côte de Bœuf to be just like that.

I managed to get a liquor license, but that did not transform the place overnight. It's not so easy to have the Paris spirit if no one working in the front of the house has ever lived there. Incredibly, my friend Eamon, who originally got me the job in Paris, was moving to Toronto with his family. It was a full circle, and I was proud and happy to give him a place to land and to pay back the opportunity and trust he had given me. He brought 25 years of living and serving in Paris with him—that effortless professional French waiter's way of saying "*bien sûr*" as he pours you another glass.

He immediately grabbed the place by the collar, ordering French wine and putting it in the window, under the shelf with the butchered meat. We got the sign artist back to add "Bar à Vin" under "Côte de Bœuf" on the front window. We got wine barrels for the front room and put zinc and wood tops on them, and built an oak bar with a zinc top and a bullnose finish and a brass footrail that I found on one of my hunts. We moved the family dinners to the back butcher table, pulling it into the middle of the room, and hung a chandelier with flickering red lights that looked like a ball of fire. My brother called the dinner space "a nook inside a nook," and it was magical. It felt like the type of loving little joint with simple, loving food you'd stumble across on a small street in Paris. As if reality were suspended while you were at Côte de Bœuf, so that when you left you felt transformed, but you weren't sure why. Those are the moments I am always striving for—when a restaurant becomes a refuge from routine and a place to recharge. And slowly but steadily, Côte de Bœuf started to clang and bang and come alive, conjuring the boisterousness of the Baron Rouge and the lovingness of Robert et Louise.

As Union and Côte de Bœuf got busier, I grew detached. I'd suspended reality so long I was running on fear. Both places had blown past my grasp and turned frantic. The throttle was too high; we were burning too much gas. Every week, something broke—fridges, stoves, drains, hood fans. Packed houses, zero profit. I said yes to everything, bled money, and mistook busyness for control. When the phone didn't ring, I froze. Silence felt wrong. Working was my only medicine—the only way to keep things feeling the same.

The circumstances of my life were catching up with me, and I was terrified to face the pain. Scared to lose people, scared to change, terrified of being unworthy, I became an avatar of myself—saying yes, avoiding conflict, wanting to be liked. I was at the whim of everyone around me, desperate for approval and completely self-conscious. Like the restaurants, I was running out of space and time to keep saying yes. I lived in my head, detached from my heart. I hid myself and felt nothing. My only expression of self was these restaurants, but all I was doing was tasking and fawning and fucking them up—no cooking, no presence, nothing.

The truth was I had no real friends because I hadn't been one. Saturdays felt empty, just like my own childhood had, with my father in bed most of the day. I struggled to fill that void and be present with my daughter. There's a photo from that time—me at the farm, afternoon, Bud Light in hand, gut hanging out. I looked like my father did when I was a kid: hunched, anxious, trapped. I was shocked to see myself like that. I knew something had to change. I couldn't keep living like that; it was death.

I know this is hard to believe—I can hardly believe it myself—but I am not making it up. That same day, I got a text from a woman named Nadia. We became friends from working on the same street. She is Anishinaabe, and she wanted to tell me about a dream she'd had about my father. She held onto it for years, until she asked an elder, who told her to share it with me. In the dream, he was talking up the restaurant, proud as ever. She'd never met him, but the way she told it—his mannerisms, his delivery, the way he would talk up my brother and me—I believed her. Feeling so lost that day, I asked if there was anywhere around her home in Sioux Lookout where I could go cook. I'd always wanted to cook in the wilderness, like my grandfather did when he went hunting. That's when she told me about Ralph's natural healing camp, WeQuenGwayWin. I texted Ralph, and he wrote back right away: "Can you come this week?" Three weeks later, I made it there.

Ralph is a 69-year-old Ojibway Anishinaabe residential school survivor. He has glasses and long grey hair with light brown highlights from the sun. He's barrel-chested and wears blue jeans that taper a bit at the bottom and black cowboy boots with silver toe tips and jingle bobs. He says "awesome" and "powerful" a lot, and "Holy Man" when something unexpected happens, and he drives a white Dodge pickup with "Pike Clan" written on the licence plate.

When I first started going to his camp to cook, I'd bring a big duffel bag full of all my hits and cooking securities—3-bone côte de bœuf, ginger cake mix, duck fat, cultured butter, galangal, Maldon salt, Yummy House soy sauce, spices, and anything else I could stuff in there: a slab of smoked bacon, maybe some duck legs—anything that would soothe my fear and nervousness. Now I just bring myself. I do a small shop at a grocery store along the way and that is it. Sometimes there are over 30 people there, sometimes even more. But either way, I have learned to trust the magic that can happen when you cook for people, and the love that transfers when you put yourself on the line. It helps that there is always some deer or moose in the freezer, and that we hunt ducks down the river, and catch fish on the way back to fry. Near the end of summer, wild rice growing along the riverbed is picked, shaken, shelled, and then roasted in a large pan under a slow-burning fire.

I roasted ducks one time with soy sauce, Five Alive juice, and some Korean red pepper powder, then went into the sweat lodge and forgot about them. I came out three hours later and ran to the oven to find them with a perfect glazed red hue—maybe a little too dark on the bottom, but amazing. I would not have been able to do that if I tried.

There is always some luck on your side when you put yourself out there. It is the best way to cook for people. To really lean into the what-ifs. To fight past the imposter syndrome and step into the unknown open spaces where anything can happen. To not hover or shy away or stress and control, but bring your whole self and be as patient as possible in the uncomfortable moments when you don't know how it will turn out. Trust me, it will be good if your heart is in it and your intention is love.

Learn to relax in that space and trust that something incredible might happen. I'm not saddled with a duffel bag anymore, full of everything I don't know or might mess up when I cook. Because I can cook with my whole self, I am never missing anything. And now I see cooking as an open space to enter, where anything can happen—and that doesn't scare me. The magic that might happen excites me more than the fear of the disaster it could be.

CÔTE DE BŒUF
130
OUVERT
CÔTE DE BŒUF
BAR À VIN
Caviste
Hot n Cold
Sandwiches to go
Take out Menu
POUSSEZ

Steak Tartare

SERVES 2

10½ oz (300 g) finely chopped beef (sirloin, eye of round, or tenderloin), cleaned of fat and sinew (ask your local butcher to do this)

1 tsp chopped curly parsley

½ tsp ground black pepper (use Brasserie Lipp pepper if you've got it)

3 Tbsp finely chopped shallot

3 Tbsp finely chopped cornichons

2 Tbsp French Dijon mustard

1½ Tbsp truffle paste (I prefer Menu brand)

4 tsp olive oil

2 tsp soy sauce

TOPPING

1 free-range egg yolk (optional)

Pinch of ground black pepper

Maldon salt

12 green peppercorns in brine

At Côte de Bœuf, we do a classic steak tartare—Paris-style, like you'd get at Brasserie Lipp. We add some Piedmont truffle paste and finish it with a raw yolk on top. It hits all the notes and then some. It's one of those transportive dishes that throws you right into all that is Paris. Serve it with French fries or duck fat toast. The French finish it with a dash of hot sauce.

In a large bowl, combine the beef with the parsley, pepper, shallot, cornichons, mustard, truffle paste, olive oil, and soy sauce. Fold the mixture over itself repeatedly until fully combined.

Gently press the tartare meat into a ring mold. Remove the mold and top with the egg yolk, if desired, pepper, a sprinkle of salt, and the green peppercorns.

French Onion Soup

SERVES 6

¾ cup butter, cubed
5 lb (2.3 kg) onions, thinly sliced (about 6 to 8 large onions)
2 tsp salt
⅓ cup cognac
⅓ cup red wine vinegar
1 cup red wine
8 cups beef stock
1 bouquet garni (bay leaf, thyme, rosemary) (see Tabac Hack)
1 Tbsp ground black pepper
6 toasted baguette slices
1½ cups grated Comté, Swiss, or any good melting cheese

We lean into this soup in the winter. It's a staple at the restaurant. Upstairs, there's a little kitchen nook where we cook the onions in a big, heavy-bottomed Rondeau. The onions slowly stew and caramelize for a couple of hours, and one of the cooks working up there will occasionally walk by and give them a stir. Then the wine goes in, along with the herbs and stock, and suddenly the whole place smells warm and loving and delicious.

My dad's mom—we called her Grandmama—opened a hotel by a lake in Haliburton in the late '70s called Hunter's Horn. It had big hallways with red carpets and a roaring fireplace. I imagine this soup being on her menu, alongside her meat pies, casseroles, and tarts, filling the dining room with her love and warmth.

TABAC HACK

To make a bouquet garni, bundle one bay leaf, a few sprigs of thyme, and a sprig of rosemary together. Tie them with kitchen twine or wrap them in a small square of cheesecloth and secure the bundle tightly.

In a large, heavy-bottomed stockpot or rondeau, melt the butter over medium-low heat. Add the onions and salt. Cook slowly, stirring every few minutes, for about 45 to 50 minutes, until deep brown and caramelized.

Add the cognac and vinegar to deglaze the pan, scraping up any browned bits with a wooden spoon. Once the liquid has evaporated, repeat the deglazing process with the wine, stirring until reduced by three-quarters.

Add the stock, bouquet garni, and pepper. Bring to a simmer and cook for 25 minutes, stirring occasionally, until it smells and tastes amazing. Taste and adjust the seasoning with more salt and pepper, if needed.

Preheat the broiler.

Ladle the soup into oven-safe bowls. Top each with a slice of baguette and ¼ cup of cheese. Broil for 2 to 4 minutes, until the cheese is melted and bubbly.

Escargots au Beurre Persillé

SERVES 2

- 1 lb (450 g) unsalted butter, softened
- 1 bunch parsley, stems removed and leaves finely chopped
- 4 large garlic cloves, minced
- 2 tsp kosher salt
- 1 tsp ground black pepper
- 1 dash Pernod liqueur
- 1 can (4.4 oz/125 g) snails in brine

When you walk into Côte de Bœuf and these are on someone's table, the smell hits you—and suddenly you're in Paris.

In a medium bowl, combine the butter, parsley, garlic, salt, pepper, and Pernod. Mix thoroughly with a rubber spatula until fully combined. Transfer to the fridge and let it firm up for about 1 hour. (Leftover parsley butter can be stored in plastic wrap in the fridge for up to 1 week—it's great on garlic bread and steak.)

Meanwhile, preheat the oven to 425°F.

Arrange the snails in two escargot dishes—one snail per well. Spoon about 1 tsp of the parsley butter over each snail.

Bake for 5 minutes, until the butter is bubbling and the dish smells delicious.

Roast Beef Sandwich

SERVES 3

- 2 lb (900 g) eye of round or inside round beef
- 2 Tbsp ground black pepper
- 1 tsp salt
- Pinch of garlic powder, or 1 garlic clove, grated
- 1 Tbsp soy sauce (I prefer Yummy House)
- 1 baguette, cut crosswise into three 6-inch pieces
- Dijon mustard
- Truffle Aioli (variation, page 285)
- 18 oz (500 g) Comté cheese, grated
- Bread-and-Butter Pickles (page 280)

In the 1980s, I worked at a butcher and fine foods shop called Michael Desborough. I helped clean turkeys for Christmas and Thanksgiving. I remember the smell of roast beef drifting through the store from the old black Garland oven in the basement. They'd cook it super rare and slice it thin for their sandwiches.

Years later, when Mike was doing the butchery at Côte de Bœuf, we started roasting beef the same way. He came up with this sandwich—roast beef, truffle aioli, and Comté cheese, all on a baguette.

Preheat the oven to 350°F.

In a roasting pan, evenly coat the beef with the pepper, salt, garlic powder, and soy sauce—just like how my grandfather used to do it. (You may need to roll the beef around for even coating).

Roast for 45 minutes. To check doneness, stab to the center of the roast with a paring knife, leave it in for a moment, then pull it out and touch the knife just above your lip. If it's warm, it's ready. If it's barely warm, give it another 10 minutes. If it's cold, it's still raw and needs another 20 minutes. Let the beef rest until cool enough to slice, 2 to 3 hours.

Use a long knife to shave the beef as thin as you can. It doesn't have to be perfect—shaving it off in scraps will keep it thin and tender.

To assemble the sandwiches, slice each baguette piece in half lengthwise. Spread a thin layer of mustard and then a thin layer of truffle aioli on the bottom halves. Pile on the sliced roast beef and season with salt and pepper. Add a generous handful of cheese on top of the beef, then a line of pickles. Smear another thin layer of truffle aioli on the top half of each baguette and close the sandwiches.

Peameal Bacon Sandwich

SERVES 4

8 thick slices challah bread

Butter

12 slices peameal bacon (store-bought or homemade; see page 174)

4 eggs

4 slices Swiss cheese

4 Rösti (page 105)

Spicy Mayo (page 286)

Bread-and-Butter Pickles (page 280)

My very first job with a paycheck was at a small grocery store around the corner from my house. I was 12 and worked weekends stocking shelves, breaking boxes in the basement, and slamming price tags on cereal boxes. It had a butcher counter in the back and a meat locker with a big wooden door, a worn-out metal latch, and sawdust on the floor. The place was called Avenue Road Food Market, but everyone called it Frank's.

Frank ran the butcher counter. He was around sixty, short and roundish, with a kind face and peaceful voice. He had an old, weathered, wrinkled butcher who helped cut meat on weekends named Ed. Frank let me back there whenever I wanted, and I would watch them break down a beef hip hanging in a small, one-windowed, wood-slabbed room behind the counter, with sawdust and dried-up beef scraps on the floor.

Afterward, I'd go pick up lunch for the curmudgeonly old cutter at the diner around the corner—peameal and home fries. Another old guy would be cooking there, and he'd load up the takeout container, thinking it was for me. I was too shy to tell him any different, and the old cutter would always be surprised by the heaps of peameal and home fries he got as he opened the box and squeezed ketchup all over them. It was a misunderstanding too complex for me to undo, but I kind of liked one old guy feeding another old guy with the same care as if it were a young, hardworking kid on his lunch break on a Saturday afternoon.

Lightly toast the bread. While it's toasting, heat a pan over medium heat and melt a bit of butter. Sear the peameal bacon for 2 to 3 minutes per side, until golden brown. Set aside.

In the same pan, fry the eggs over medium heat. You can break the yolks slightly if you prefer, but keep them soft and runny.

CONTINUES

To build each sandwich, place a few slices of bacon on one slice of toasted bread, followed by the Swiss cheese. Add the fried egg on top, then the rösti, and finish with a little spicy mayo and some pickles. Close the sandwich, slice in half, and serve immediately.

HOMEMADE PEAMEAL BACON

MAKES 12 TO 16 SLICES

- 8 cups water
- ¾ cup kosher salt
- ½ cup white sugar
- 3 Tbsp pickling spice
- 3 Tbsp brown sugar
- 2 Tbsp honey
- Handful of ice
- 1 tsp pink salt (optional)
- 1 pork loin (2 lb/900 g, 6 to 8 inches long)
- Polenta, for coating

TABAC HACK

Place a small plate on top of the pork and fill a container with water to place on top of the plate, to serve as a weight to keep the pork fully immersed in the brine.

For dinner, my grandmother would roast a peameal bacon loin with an inch of water in the bottom of the roasting pan and serve it with her chunk pickle and Nance's Mustard that she'd get in Florida.

In a large pot, bring the water, kosher salt, white sugar, pickling spice, brown sugar, and honey to a boil for a few minutes (think of it like steeping tea). Don't add the pink salt yet. Once it's off the heat, toss in the ice to help it cool down quickly, then stir in the pink salt (if using).

While the brine's coming down to room temp, poke your pork loin a few times with a paring knife so the brine can penetrate more easily.

Put the pork loin in a container and pour the cooled brine over it, making sure it's fully submerged (see Tabac Hack). Cover the container with a lid or plastic wrap and let it sit in the brine for 4 days in the fridge.

After brining, spread some polenta on a tray and roll the pork in it so it's completely coated. Store it in an airtight container in the fridge for up to 10 days. Cut off ½-inch slices as you're ready to eat them.

County Terrine Sandwich

SERVES 6

PANADE

2 large eggs, beaten

¾ cup heavy (35%) cream

2 Tbsp whisky (scotch, bourbon—whatever's hiding in the cabinet; red wine or vinegar work too)

1 slice white or sourdough bread, ripped into small pieces

PÂTÉ SPICE

2 Tbsp ground allspice

½ tsp ground nutmeg

½ tsp ground cinnamon

½ tsp ground cloves

COUNTY TERRINE

2¼ lb (1 kg) ground pork

10½ oz (300 g) shredded corned beef

1 shallot, diced

1 garlic clove, grated

1½ tsp salt

1 tsp ground black pepper

1½ tsp pâté spice

1 tsp duck fat

TO SERVE

6 favorite buns

Spicy Mayo (page 286)

Bread-and-Butter Pickles (page 280)

Grainy triple crunch mustard (I like Kozlik's)

Butter lettuce

Habanero Sauce (page 288)

There's a guy I bump into now and then, and he always asks when the terrine sandwich is coming back to Côte de Bœuf. I don't think we ever made a headcheese sandwich, but I'm guessing he means this one. It hits all the notes, with chunks of corned beef cooked into a terrine, then sliced and seared on the flat-top so it gets golden and crispy. It's like a gourmet meatloaf sandwich with triple crunch mustard, spiced mayo, and lettuce. It's great with a fried egg too.

Preheat the oven to 350°F.

MAKE THE PANADE: In a medium bowl, whisk the eggs, cream, and whisky. Add the torn bread and let it soak for 10 to 15 minutes, until the liquid is fully absorbed. This is the binder that holds the terrine together.

MAKE THE PÂTÉ SPICE: Meanwhile, in a small bowl, combine the allspice, nutmeg, cinnamon, and cloves.

MAKE THE TERRINE: In a large bowl, combine the ground pork, corned beef, shallot, garlic, salt, pepper, and pâté spice. Add the panade and mix with your hands until just combined. You want visible chunks of white fat and threads of corned beef running through.

Line a small terrine dish or loaf pan with plastic wrap. Pack in the terrine mixture, pressing it into the corners, and fold the plastic over the top.

Set the pan in a larger roasting pan and pour in hot water to come halfway up the sides. Bake for 1 hour, until the internal temperature reaches 160°F. It should puff slightly, like a meatloaf. Let the terrine rest in the pan for 1 hour.

CONTINUES

TABAC HACK

Heritage pigs often have a thick layer of fat on their chops—most butchers will have some on hand. You can buy a piece and salt it overnight in the fridge (1 tsp salt per 3½ oz/100 g pork). The next day, rinse, cube, and fold it into the terrine mixture.

Unwrap the terrine and slice it into 1-inch-thick pieces. In a skillet, heat the duck fat over medium heat and sear the slices for about 3 minutes per side, until golden brown.

TO SERVE: Split the buns and spread the bottoms with spicy mayo. Add a slice of warm terrine, then layer on pickles, triple crunch mustard, butter lettuce, and a few drops of habanero sauce. Cap with the top bun and serve.

Sichuan Chicken Club Sandwich

MAKES 2 SANDWICHES

12 oz (340 g) pulled roast chicken
Juice of 1 lime
1 Tbsp soy sauce
1 Tbsp mirin (I like Honteri brand)
1 Tbsp mayonnaise
1 tsp sambal oelek
½ tsp toasted sesame oil
Salt and ground black pepper
Handful of Thai basil leaves, chopped
8 slices bacon
6 slices white bread
Softened butter
1 tomato, sliced
Butter lettuce leaves

TABAC HACK

If you have Spicy Mayo (page 286) in your pantry, sub it in for the sambal, mirin, and mayo.

We used to make these at Côte de Bœuf with the leftover roast chickens from the window. We'd pull the meat and toss it with sesame oil, soy, sambal, lime juice, and Thai basil. It turns into a bold, punchy chicken salad that forms the base of the sandwich. Layer it with bacon, tomato, lettuce, and toasted white bread, and you've got a proper club. It's the kind of move you make on a lazy Sunday with whatever roast chicken you've got lying around, like the Barbecued Peking Chicken (page 183).

Place the pulled chicken in a medium bowl. Add the lime juice, soy sauce, mirin, mayonnaise, sambal oelek, and sesame oil. Season with a pinch of salt and a few cracks of black pepper. Mix everything thoroughly. Gently fold in the Thai basil. Taste and adjust the seasoning, if needed.

In a pan over medium heat, cook the bacon until crisp. Transfer to a paper towel–lined plate to drain.

Toast the bread until golden brown. While the toast is still warm, spread a thin layer of butter on one side of each slice.

To assemble, place one slice of toast on a cutting board, buttered side up. Add a generous scoop of the chicken mixture, spreading it evenly. Top with two slices of bacon and a few slices of tomato. Place a second slice of toast on top, buttered side up. Top with another scoop of chicken and some lettuce. Finish with the final slice of toast, buttered side down. Press the sandwich gently to hold everything together, and slice into four quarters. Repeat with the remaining ingredients to make the second sandwich.

Divorce Lasagna

SERVES 6

2¼ lb (1 kg) 00 flour
12 large egg yolks
2 large whole eggs
1 Tbsp apple cider vinegar
1 Tbsp olive oil
Pinch of salt
2 batches Béchamel Sauce (page 31)
4 Tbsp truffle paste
1 batch Bolognese Sauce (page 77)
2 cups grated Comté, Piave, or Parmesan cheese (enough to cover the top)

We made this lasagna at Côte de Bœuf during the pandemic, using Union's Bolognese sauce. Two kitchens, one dish. We added truffle paste to the béchamel and used Comté cheese. We were just scraping by, like everyone else, and selling this lasagna for $30. It was just big enough for two people, but the cost—at a time when everyone was strapped and scared—caused a few fiscal standoffs between husbands and wives. Pretty soon, it picked up a nickname around the neighborhood: divorce lasagna.

You can use homemade pasta or store-bought sheets. If you've still got a pasta roller kicking around from the 1990s, I've included a pasta recipe here—I learned it from Michael Stadtlander.

Pour the flour into a large bowl and make a well in the center. Add the egg yolks, whole eggs, vinegar, olive oil, and salt. Mix the eggs gently, then begin folding in the flour with your hands. Knead until the dough forms a firm, smooth ball—no dry flakes, no sticky mess. If it's too dry, wet your hands slightly and knead again. A flaky dough will crack in the roller (and upset you).

Cut the dough in half, wrap each piece in plastic wrap, and chill for 1 hour.

Remove one dough ball from the fridge and flatten it with a rolling pin until it's about 1 inch thick. Start feeding it through the pasta roller at the widest setting (usually #6). Run it through twice. Move to setting #5 and roll twice, then setting #4, also twice. Finish with one pass each through settings #3 and #2. Cut the dough into six sheets, each roughly 6 × 12 inches, and lay them on a cornmeal-dusted baking sheet so they don't stick. Repeat with the second dough ball.

Preheat the oven to 375°F.

To the béchamel sauce, stir in the truffle paste.

CONTINUES

ASSEMBLE THE LASAGNA: In a 9 × 13-inch baking dish, lay down two sheets of pasta, side by side. Spoon on some Bolognese sauce. (Go easy. The key to a good lasagna is to use less filling—it's all about balance between the pasta and the sauce.) Continue layering pasta and Bolognese in this way, keeping the layers restrained, until you have five layers of pasta, finishing with pasta on top. Then a layer of truffle béchamel. Top it off with a good whack of cheese.

Cover with foil. Bake for 1 hour, until piping hot. For the last 10 minutes, take the foil off to let the top brown.

Barbecued Peking Chicken

SERVES 4

CURE MIX

¾ cup packed golden brown sugar

½ cup kosher flake salt

1 whole chicken (about 4 lb/1.8 kg)

¼ cup pure maple syrup

¼ cup good-quality olive oil (I like Alhema)

1 tsp ground black pepper

Chicken stock, for deglazing

1 tsp Hotel Butter (page 283)

My friend Nathan lives down the road from my family farm. He used to raise chickens all summer and sell them on a fall Friday night with beer and snacks. Thick-skinned, plump, beautiful birds, raised on his homemade feed mix. One time, he had a couple of birds left over, so I gave him this recipe. He loved it. "It was so juicy, I stuck my fork in and the juice shot out and hit me right in the eye—*right in my eye!*" he exclaimed.

The cure opens up the skin at the molecular level, so the juice doesn't leak out but fills the bird instead. It also makes the bird plump and gives it a reddish hue, so it looks like Peking duck. Expect smoky, salty, and sweet flavors, tried and tested by an awesome guy. Serve with Smashed Potatoes (page 271).

MAKE THE CURE MIX: In a large bowl, using your hands, mix the brown sugar and salt thoroughly.

Rub the cure all over the chicken, getting into the crevices, especially under the wings and around the legs. Place the chicken skin side up on a tray. Cover and refrigerate for about 4 hours, then turn it so the skin side is down in the cure juices and let the legs get some time in the cure too. If you can, leave it overnight in the fridge, turning it occasionally so all sides of the bird get attention.

When you're ready to cook, rinse off the cure and pat the bird dry with paper towels.

In a small bowl, combine the maple syrup, olive oil, and pepper.

Set the chicken on a clean tray and drizzle with the maple syrup mixture. Rub everything in well. The bird is now ready for the grill or a hot smoker.

CONTINUES

Barbecue or smoke the chicken over indirect heat (if smoking, I like apple or cherry wood). After about 1 hour, check the bird—it should be golden and beautiful.

Meanwhile, preheat the oven to 400°F.

Transfer the chicken to a roasting pan and roast in the preheated oven for 20 minutes, until the internal temperature registers 165°F. Transfer the chicken to a cutting board to rest. Once rested, carve the chicken into quarters by separating the legs at the joint, then cutting the breast in half on the diagonal.

Place the roasting pan on the stovetop over medium heat, add a splash of chicken stock, and get it boiling, scraping up the browned bits from the bottom of the pan, for 1 minute, until slightly reduced. Stir in the hotel butter to finish the sauce. Serve the pan sauce alongside the chicken.

Côte de Bœuf *with* Peppercorn Sauce and Pommes Sautées

SERVES 3 TO 4

CÔTE DE BŒUF

2½ to 3½ lb (1.1 to 1.6 kg) côte de bœuf (bone-in rib steak, see Tabac Hack)

Kosher salt and ground black pepper

1 Tbsp duck fat or beef tallow

FLASH PAN PEPPERCORN SAUCE

2 Tbsp butter

1 shallot, diced

¼ cup port

Scant ½ cup heavy (35%) cream

1 Tbsp Better Than Bouillon beef base

1 Tbsp green peppercorns, plus more for cracking

POMMES SAUTÉES

5 Russet potatoes, boiled whole, with skin on, until almost falling apart

2 Tbsp duck fat, plus more if needed

Salt and ground black pepper

TO SERVE

1 Tbsp Hotel Butter (page 283)

Robert et Louise is a place in Paris on rue Vieille du Temple. It's an old, family-run stone and wood tavern with checkered tablecloths, boudin noir with sautéed apples, and big, amazing côtes de bœuf cooked in the old fireplace nestled into the back wall, amongst the tables and chairs. A plank of wood juts out into the room and is slowly pushed into the fire, serving as a consistent heat source under a flat cast-iron skillet to cook the côtes de bœuf. The skillet gives the côte a golden salt and pepper crust as it cooks in its own fat. When I went, the niece was cooking the beef and slicing it onto wooden boards. Off to the side, in a kitchen nook, the aunts were cooking the pommes sautées. It felt like you were in a family home, with all the chaos and drama of life happening around a crescendo of cooking and serving. Family staff wove through the tables and chairs with a vibe of *Why are all these people in my way? Oh right, we invited them.*

Hold on to that Robert et Louise vision—the hearth, the spirit—when you cook this côte de bœuf. Lean into it.

COOK THE CÔTE DE BŒUF: Season the beef generously with salt and pepper. (I channel an old French guy or a loving aunt for this part—whatever works. Just season it with authority and love.)

Heat a 12-inch cast-iron skillet over medium heat. Add the duck fat. Once the fat is hot, sear the beef on one side for 7 to 10 minutes. Keep the heat steady—not screaming hot, though. Flip and repeat on the other side. The cooking time will vary depending on the age of the meat. I've cooked enough of these that I can pick it up and feel the doneness—the beef gets lighter as it cooks through. If it still has the same weight as it did when it hit the pan, it's still raw in the middle. You're going for an internal temperature of about 125°F; it'll rise to around 130°F as it rests. Pull it off and let it rest uncovered for 15 to 20 minutes.

CONTINUES

TABAC HACKS

If you've got gray salt from Brittany, use it.

The rib bone doesn't need to be as long as we butcher it at Côte de Bœuf. A 2-inch bone from the ribeye works, so you can fit it in your pan.

It's important to have a hot platter because the beef has been resting for 15 minutes. Between the warm platter and hot peppercorn sauce, it'll be perfect.

MAKE THE SAUCE: In the same skillet, melt the butter over medium heat. Add the shallot and sauté briefly, scraping up the bits with a spatula. Splash in the port and let it simmer for a moment. Stir in the cream, beef base, and green peppercorns. Bring to a simmer, then crack in more green pepper.

COOK THE SAUTÉES: While the beef rests, peel the skins off the boiled potatoes by hand and break them into large chunks.

In a large pan, heat the duck fat over medium heat. Add the potatoes in a single layer; they should sizzle. Keep adding the potatoes until the pan is full. It's fine if a few pieces are piled on each other (they'll get their turn eventually). Let them sizzle undisturbed for a few minutes, then begin turning and flipping them over to incorporate the ones on top. Season generously with salt and pepper. Keep sautéing for 10 to 15 minutes, adding more fat if needed, until the potatoes are golden and crisp on the outside and fluffy in the middle. (If they hold together in perfect pieces when you cut them, they have not been cooked enough.) These should be served immediately—timing is important here.

FINISH THE STEAK: Transfer the beef to a cutting board. With one hand holding the bone steady, slice parallel to it, starting from the outer edge of the steak and cutting inward until you reach the bone.

Arrange the sliced beef on a preheated platter (see Tabac Hack). Season with a bit more salt and pepper. Serve with the hot pommes sautées in the pan, and top with hotel butter.

TAMA

Tamworth Pork Chop *with* Creamy Mustard Green Peppercorn Sauce

SERVES 2

- 2 heritage pork chops (each about 12 oz/340 g and about 1 inch thick; go to your butcher for these)
- Salt and ground black pepper
- 1 tsp Korean ground red pepper (gochugaru), divided
- 1 tsp duck fat or olive oil
- 2 shallots, sliced into rounds
- Splash of cognac
- ¼ cup water
- 1 heaping tsp green peppercorns in brine
- 1 tsp Better Than Bouillon beef base
- ⅓ cup heavy (35%) cream
- 1 tsp Dijon mustard
- ½ tsp pure maple syrup

TABAC HACK

Once the pork comes out of the pan, don't pour off the excess fat, but sauté 1 pint of sliced cremini mushrooms. Then continue with the shallots, cognac, etc.

Damien gets sides of Tamworth pigs at Côte de Bœuf about every 2 weeks. They have a fat cap an inch thick. We salt the fat and use it for terrines or render it down for scrunchions to cook fresh cod with. There's just something about a pork chop in a pan with a creamy mustard sauce that hits. The fat gets golden, and the flesh stays pink, with a salt and pepper crust. The pan can be deglazed with a hit of cognac and turned into something like a French country sauce. You'll be transported to an unexpected spot in the French countryside. Serve with the Pommes Sautées (page 187).

Choose a heavy-bottomed skillet or frying pan wide enough to fit both pork chops. Heat the pan to medium heat so the pork sizzles when it hits the pan.

Season the pork chops generously with salt, black pepper, and half of the Korean pepper. Add the duck fat to the hot pan. (The fat from the pork will do most of the work.) Sear the chops for 7 to 9 minutes on the first side, until the fat crisps and caramelizes. Flip and cook for another 5 to 7 minutes, depending on the thickness, until just a hint of pink remains inside the pork. Remove the chops from the pan and set aside.

If there's a pool of fat left in the pan, pour off the excess (see Tabac Hack). Toss in the shallots and sauté for a minute. Deglaze with a splash of cognac, scraping up the browned bits. Stir in the water, peppercorns, and bouillon until combined, then stir in the cream and mustard. Simmer for 1 minute. Finish with the remaining ½ tsp Korean pepper and maple syrup.

Serve the pork chops with the sauce spooned over top.

Mousse au Chocolat *with* Sea Salt

SERVES 8

- 13.4 oz (380 g) good-quality dark chocolate chips (70% cocoa)
- 2⅔ cups heavy (35%) cream, divided
- 5 eggs, yolks and whites separated, divided
- ¾ cups white sugar, divided
- Pinch of salt
- Maldon salt, to finish

I'm not much of a baker—I tend to wing it, which doesn't always fly when precision matters. So I search out desserts like this, especially for dinners. It's easy to execute and always a big hit. This one's from Côte de Bœuf and has been on the menu since day one.

To execute this seamlessly, you're going to need four bowls because you're melting chocolate, whipping cream, whisking egg yolks, and beating egg whites all separately.

In a heatproof bowl, combine the chocolate chips and 1⅓ cups of the cream. Place over simmering water in a double boiler on medium-low heat. Stir until melted and smooth, then remove from the heat and set aside.

Turn off the heat but keep the pot of hot water on the stove. Set a clean heatproof bowl over the hot water to create a bain-marie. Add the egg yolks, half the sugar, and the salt to the bowl. Whisk continuously until the mixture becomes thick, pale, and creamy with no streaks of dark yellow.

Fold in the chocolate mixture until smooth. Set aside.

In a large bowl, whip the remaining 1⅓ cups cream with the remaining sugar until soft peaks form.

In a separate bowl, beat the egg whites into stiff peaks, but don't over-whip.

Using a spatula, gently fold the whipped cream into the chocolate mixture until combined. Then gently fold in the meringue, a little at a time, until combined.

Portion the mousse into ramekins. Refrigerate for 2 hours. When serving, finish each portion with a pinch of Maldon salt.

CÔTE

Dining Lounge
Hearth's

Heart's

Heart's

When I was a kid, my dad used to take us to a restaurant called Hart's. I remember there being a big glass bowl of cinnamon heart candies at the corner of the wood bar, and checkered tablecloths on the square tables in the back. It was a bar-restaurant-tavern kind of place that served chicken wings, burgers, and steak and had specials every night. It had the classic restaurant layout, with a swinging door leading into the kitchen in the back. After eating there, we'd go to the movies at the theater around the corner. My dad loved to recount how the Queen rolled by Hart's one time as he was enjoying lunch.

Restaurants were where my father felt most comfortable and was his best self. He named my younger brother, Chasen, after a restaurant in LA. Everyone knew and loved him, and we felt special being in his family. He was funny and witty and generous, and had a smile and humility that put people at ease. Servers were treated like friends, and they'd all come by and say hi and laugh, and he'd joke with them, asking what they'd been up to.

Nestled in booths—amongst the hustle, the muffled voices, and the clatter of glasses—was where we shared our best moments as a family. Eating out was our specialty. Restaurants welcomed us in from the noise and anxiety of the city, and I loved the ease and togetherness of it. It was exciting and fun, and a reprieve from the heaviness I felt at home. But after the meal, when we got home, the din and magic of the restaurant would fade.

❖

My parents doubled down and purchased our family farm in the 1980s, and it took everything they had. They drove a beat-up, old light blue Chevy Malibu wagon, which would break down along the highway every few trips.

An old tavern that served cabbage rolls and perogies went up for sale by the family farm a few years ago. Having been up there since I was a kid, I wasn't sure I wanted to start a business there, but my friend Tyler, who'd worked at Union, had fresh eyes on the area and convinced me to go for it together. It was cheap and decrepit and worth a shot. It has one of those "pull into" parking lots, and I called it Heart's—a quiet nod to the place my dad used to take us.

Heart's is a Pep kind of place. Pep is a big burly Catalan man I met in Girona when Chris and I cooked a dinner there for a group of cyclists. He loves his town, drinks cava out of a jug with a spout so it pours into his mouth when he holds it over his head. He enters wild boar contests every year and drives around with jamon and cava in his trunk just in case he meets a group of cyclists on the road so after a gruelling climb he can offer it to them. After I showed him a picture of my smokehouse, he promptly went home and built his own. So when I think about Heart's, I think about Pep, with its tavern feel and stone-walled open cellar and big wooden table and smokehouse and chickens and a big garden in the back for vegetables.

From building the other two spots and cooking at Ralph's camp, I'd learned to let things reveal themselves and not push them through too quickly just for the sake of it. Heart's was a long, painful build during the pandemic, but the uncomfortable time allowed space for it to reveal itself and for its tavern-like spirit to show up and we got it done. I've learned that a restaurant doesn't have to be perfect at the start; some answers need time—and guests flowing in—to help you pinpoint what needs to be done. It's about keeping your intention in your mind, and ours was a roadside tavern. So when you walk in, there are barrel-top tables, and a horseshoe bar, and an open kitchen on the other side, and a lot of good food with a tavern force, and really good wine.

Working there doesn't feel like work. Heart's doesn't have the usual restaurant traps that make your brain melt; it has flow.

It is a tavern in the front with a farmhouse in the back attached by the enclosed porch we call the "train car" room. During the build, the rotting basement ceiling got blown open at the back of the house and it exposed the stone foundation from the first floor, and became the cellar room with a big, long table. We had already stripped the place down to the hemlock walls and original floors that still had a country paint. And when those beautiful stone walls came into focus underneath, it was like uncovering a masterpiece—the real essence of the place. No matter how hard the build became afterward, it just felt like it would be okay when it was done. The cellar makes me think of Piedmont and the food made there, the simplicity, playfulness, freedom, goodness, and joy of it.

When we're building a place, we bring with us our memories, and what we choose to make with them has lasting effects. In a sense, we've been working on the build our whole lives. Tyler's dad took over a funeral home and turned it into a successful pub in Calgary, and at Heart's there are tones and touches that speak to his place. Everywhere I went, I was looking for home, and everything I gathered along the way were pieces of a longing to make sense of it all. I'm still working on that, but I know I can find comfort in the memories of beautiful places and people. The paintings my grandparents had in their basement lounge, where they used to listen to the radio and play records and drink scotch and entertain, have found a new home at Heart's. They have looked out of place everywhere else since they left that basement, but they seem to work on these walls. A lot of things have found homes here. A place to pull into and be fed and nourished by a culmination of memories, experiences, and everything gathered and carried along the way.

An amazing thing happened after we opened. A lady drove by and decided to come in for lunch—it was a Sunday. She sat in the train car room. When Annie, who manages the place, was taking her order, the lady told her that the place really reminded her of her dad's place. Annie said, "Oh yeah, it was inspired by a place called Hart's." The woman started crying and said that was her dad's place. He had passed away a few years earlier. So this is what I am talking about. When you take big chances and are bold with intention and love, there is always magic on your side. And cooking, and Heart's, is magic.

BEER
WINE
OYSTERS
Cold

Lounge

the
Village Inn
AIR CONDITIONED

CEDAR WAXWINGS 104

Romaine and Escarole Salad *with* Garlic Anchovy Dressing

SERVES 4 TO 6

- ½ baguette
- ¼ cup olive oil
- Salt and ground black pepper
- 2 garlic cloves, grated
- 2 Tbsp freshly squeezed lemon juice
- 1 heaping tsp Dijon mustard
- 1 tsp anchovy sauce
- 1 tsp honey
- ⅓ cup canola oil
- 1 head romaine lettuce
- 1 head escarole
- Hard sheep cheese (I like Zacharie Cloutier, or use a Manchego or Pecorino)

I had this salad in Baltimore at Le Comptoir du Vin, a bold, youthful micro-restaurant with a chalkboard menu, natural wine, the whole vibe. The salad was sharp and tasty, but the thing that made it was an Italian anchovy fish sauce they were selling in small bottles at the bar. Think elegant, intense, refined fish sauce with depth.

Preheat the oven to 375°F.

Cut the baguette into 1-inch cubes. On a baking sheet, toss the bread cubes with the olive oil and salt and pepper to taste, then spread out in a single layer. Bake for 5 to 7 minutes, giving them a shake around the 4-minute mark, until golden and crunchy.

In a small bowl (but big enough to get a whisk moving), whisk together the garlic, lemon juice, mustard, anchovy sauce, and honey. Slowly drizzle in the canola oil, whisking to emulsify.

Rip up the romaine and escarole and place them in a large bowl. Pour in the dressing, then add the croutons. Season with salt and pepper. Channeling that old-person, loving force and conviction, toss the salad.

The best way to plate a salad, from a visual perspective, is to stay in the middle of the bowl or plate, within the inside rim, and build upward. After plating, use a peeler to shave a generous amount of sheep cheese over each portion.

Grey Owl Endive Salad *with* Mustard Vinaigrette and Fresh Dill

SERVES 6

MUSTARD VINAIGRETTE

½ shallot, finely diced

3 Tbsp olive or canola oil

1 Tbsp Dijon mustard

1 tsp red wine vinegar or white balsamic vinegar

½ tsp honey (skip this if you're using white balsamic vinegar)

Squeeze of lemon juice

Salt and ground black pepper

SALAD

2 heads endive, roughly chopped

1 head radicchio, roughly chopped

1 bunch radishes with tops, radishes quartered and greens roughly chopped

1 Honeycrisp apple or Bartlett pear, sliced

¼ cup chopped fresh dill

½ cup pecan or walnut halves, toasted (see Tabac Hack)

7 oz (200 g) Grey Owl goat cheese or Château de Bourgogne

TABAC HACK

To toast pecan or walnut halves, spread them on a parchment-lined baking sheet and toast in a 400°F oven for 6 minutes. Spread them out on a plate to cool.

When I make a salad, I tap into my old Frenchman. I imagine my Parisian friend Pierre's dad making a simple salad for his family in a beautiful old apartment on the Left Bank. There is a gentle force a good salad needs to reach its full potential. It gets overlooked. Salad is often so simple, so last-minute, that people rush through it or forget it entirely. But you need to be present when you make a salad and see it all the way through. Taste as you go. Season. Sometimes it needs more vinaigrette, sometimes less.

Grey Owl is a great ash-rind goat cheese from Quebec—bold, striking, and truly unforgettable.

MAKE THE VINAIGRETTE: In a shallow bowl, combine the shallot, oil, mustard, vinegar, and honey (if using). Whisk until emulsified. Add a squeeze of lemon juice and whisk again. Season with salt and pepper to taste.

MAKE THE SALAD: In a large bowl, combine the endive, radicchio, radishes, radish greens, apple, and dill. Add the vinaigrette to coat lightly and toss well.

Plate the salad and finish with the pecans and Grey Owl over top.

Tuna Sashimi *with* Honey and Thyme Soy Glaze

SERVES 6 TO 8

- Sushi-grade tuna steak (about 1½ lb/700 g and about 2 inches thick, without sinew if possible) (see Tabac Hack)
- 1 tsp sugar
- ½ tsp honey
- 2 Tbsp fresh thyme leaves (see Tabac Hack)
- 2 Tbsp soy sauce
- 1 tsp mirin (I like Honteri brand)
- Good squeeze of lime juice
- 1 tsp olive oil
- Sprinkle of sea salt

TABAC HACK

You can buy frozen sushi-grade tuna steaks at most Japanese specialty stores.

If the thyme stalks are woody and tough, strip off the leaves first. But if they're thin and soft, just chop the whole thing.

I was at a fish shop in Prince Edward Island once when they hauled in a huge tuna straight from the ocean. The place we were staying had thyme growing wild through the grass by the sea, which inspired me to make this glaze to go over the raw tuna.

Slice the tuna against the grain into pieces roughly ¾ inch thick (it should look like sushi). Lay the slices on a platter and refrigerate.

In a small saucepan over medium heat, combine the sugar, honey, and ½ tsp water (the water helps caramelize the sugar more gracefully) to create a wet sand effect. Watching constantly, let the sugar melt. Once it starts to turn golden, throw in the thyme. Let it bubble up for a second or two, and just before it goes too brown, add the soy sauce and mirin, stirring to combine. Bring to a quick boil for a few seconds, then take it off the heat and set aside. It will thicken as it sits.

Once the glaze is cooled down, take the tuna out of the fridge. Drizzle the glaze generously over the tuna slices. Squeeze the lime juice all over and drizzle with the olive oil. Finish with sea salt.

Calabrian Zucchini Flower Fritters

SERVES 6 TO 8

12 or more zucchini flowers (squash blossoms work too)

1 cup flour

1 tsp salt

1 egg

½ cup water

1 zucchini, halved and thinly sliced

½ cup Parmigiano Reggiano, grated

1 tsp minced garlic

Handful of chopped Italian parsley

1 cup canola oil, for frying

As my friend Dara says, Nanci brings a lot in a little package. She's fiery, wise, full of compassion and love—and she cooks with a celebratory force that's both grounding and starry. She's Dara's best friend and a regular at the Galaxy Farm, which is a hop, skip, and a jump from Heart's. She came up for the roast duck dinner (page 223) with some zucchini flowers she'd frozen and saved from summer, made her mother's Calabrian pitti, and then fresh pasta for pho the next day. I asked if I could put the recipe in the book because it's the one that best captures the magic I'm always trying to express: what happens when you cook with your heart.

With your fingers, remove the burst stem from inside the zucchini flowers. Try to keep the flowers whole and set them aside.

In a medium bowl, whisk together the flour and salt. In a separate bowl, beat the egg and water, then pour that mixture into the flour. Stir until you get a pancake-like batter. You might need to adjust with a touch more flour or water.

Fold in the sliced zucchini, zucchini flowers, Parmigiano Reggiano, garlic, and parsley. The batter should be on the thicker side, sturdy enough to hold together when spooned.

Heat the canola oil in a cast-iron or other heavy-bottomed pan over medium-high heat to about 370°F. When the oil is hot enough, spoon in the batter—about a heaping tablespoon should do. Fry until golden on one side, about 3 minutes, then flip and cook the other side until evenly browned, about 3 minutes more.

Transfer the fritters to a paper towel–lined platter to drain. Keep going until all the batter's done. Serve warm—or at room temperature. They're just as good the next day.

Irish Soda Bread *with* Squid Ink Butter

MAKES 2 LOAVES AND 1 CUP BUTTER

SODA BREAD
2½ cups all-purpose flour
2½ cups whole wheat flour
1½ cups rolled oats
1½ Tbsp salt
1 Tbsp baking soda
2 cups buttermilk
½ cup fancy molasses
1 Tbsp honey

SQUID INK BUTTER
½ lb (225 g) butter, cubed
3 Tbsp squid ink
2 Tbsp heavy (35%) cream
2 Tbsp olive oil
Pinch of grated garlic
Salt and ground black pepper

Arlequin Tapenade (page 214)

Ross brought this bread—he calls it treacle bread—to Union when he came over from London with his wife 14 years ago. He's the OG among the three New Zealand chefs. He convinced Hamish to come over a couple years later, and Fady must have just felt the New Zealand connection; one day he walked into Le Tambour, and that was that. This bread's become a staple on the flat-top breakfasts. It's easy to make, and just as good for tartines. Toasted with butter or fried in a pan with some squid ink butter and tapenade, it's a winner.

As for the squid ink butter, I came up with that at Heart's. It just felt like the kind of place that should have it. I wanted to hit a note with it not being your usual roadside place in the country, and this just came to me. My family came in from Montreal, and one of them said, "You had me at squid ink butter." Right on.

MAKE THE BREAD: Preheat the oven to 350°F. Line a baking sheet with parchment paper.

In a large bowl, whisk together the all-purpose flour, whole wheat flour, oats, salt, and baking soda until evenly combined.

In a separate bowl, whisk the buttermilk, molasses, and honey until smooth. Pour the wet mix into the dry. Use your hands to mix, but don't overwork it.

Divide the dough in half and shape into two rough rounds. Place them on the prepared baking sheet.

Bake for 1 hour. Flip them over and knock on the bottoms—if they sound hollow and feel lighter (less dense), they're done. Or check by inserting a knife to see if it comes out clean. If not, give the loaves a few more minutes and test again. Transfer the loaves from the pan to a wire rack to cool.

CONTINUES

TABAC HACK

At Heart's, we fry the bread in duck fat on the flat-top—it's quite delicious. You can do this with your leftover bread, or you can just toast it.

MAKE THE SQUID INK BUTTER: While the bread is baking, toss the butter into a food processor. Add the squid ink, cream, olive oil, garlic, and salt and pepper to taste. Blend until smooth and whipped. Taste and check for salt. You might want more squid ink, depending on preference.

Slice the freshly baked bread and serve with the butter and tapenade. Wrap the bread in plastic wrap and store in the fridge for up to 1 week.

ARLEQUIN TAPENADE

MAKES 2 CUPS

- 1 cup pitted drained Niçoise olives (or a nice green olive)
- 1 cup pitted cured black olives
- 2 Tbsp drained capers
- 4 cured anchovies, chopped
- 1 garlic clove
- 2 Tbsp olive oil

This spread was the first thing I learned to cook from a real restaurant, when I was around 17. I immediately went to my grandparents' place and made it on toast as an hors d'oeuvre, and we sat on the slab-stoned veranda by the crabapple tree and their 1940s pool. They were impressed—it's a memory I've carried ever since. But just remember, the better the olives and anchovies, the better this will be. It's perfect with the soda bread.

In a blender, combine the Niçoise olives, black olives, capers, anchovies (if using), garlic, and olive oil. Pulse until it looks like caviar—not smooth, just broken down and a little chunky. (Heads up: You'll notice there is a pit in the blender. It always happens.)

If not serving the tapenade right away, transfer it to an airtight container and store in the fridge for up to 2 weeks.

TABAC HACK

To serve as an hors d'oeuvre, slice a baguette and toast in a pan or toaster. Rub one side of each slice with raw garlic and smear the tapenade over top.

Heart's Smash Burger *with* Truffle Aioli, Comté, and Triple Crunch

MAKES 6 BURGERS

2 lb (900 g) ground beef chuck

Salt and ground black pepper

1 tsp duck fat

3½ oz (100 g) Comté cheese (or Cantel works too), grated

6 burger buns

Truffle Aioli variation, (page 285)

Iceberg lettuce

Bread-and-Butter Pickles (page 280)

Grainy triple crunch mustard (I like Kozlik's)

When I lived in Piedmont, I helped a family cook Easter lunch for a hundred people at a banquet hall in Rodello. One of the dishes was carne cruda. The father sliced a tremendous amount of rare beef and laid it out on trays. The meat was dressed with truffle paste, olive oil, lemon, and salt. Then the cousins and daughters swooped in and rushed the trays out to the long tables packed with families. It was hard to get into these kitchens because most were family-run, and they didn't need the help or want the intrusion. But this place let me in once in a while, and I loved every minute of it.

One day they sent me to the pantry to grab something, and I found the truffle paste. I wrote the name down. Years later, I ordered it for the restaurants. We mixed it with aioli at Côte de Bœuf for the roast beef sandwiches we do at lunch. This is a burger version of that roast beef sandwich, born from an Easter lunch in Piedmont.

Portion the beef into six balls. Place the balls on a tray and season generously with salt and pepper. (Cake pans work well here; you can roll the meat around without flinging seasoning everywhere.)

Heat a pan or skillet over medium heat and add the duck fat. Place three meatballs in the pan and smash down firmly with a spatula until smash-burger flat. Cook for 5 minutes without touching them, then flip the patties. You want to see a dark, crusty sear. Add a generous amount of cheese on top. Let it melt and spread over the edges. The cheese should hit the pan and crisp into a lacy edge. Cook for another 3 minutes. Repeat with the remaining three meatballs and cheese.

Meanwhile, warm the buns in a 350°F oven. They should be soft and hot inside when they come out.

Place each burger patty on the bottom half of a bun. Smear the top half with truffle aioli, then add lettuce and a few pickles. Dollop mustard right on the patty. Close the burger and press it down gently.

Seared Cod *with* Brown Butter Sherry Vinaigrette and Scrunchions

SERVES 4

BROWN BUTTER SHERRY VINAIGRETTE

4 oz (120 g) butter

1 tsp sherry vinegar

1 tsp fresh lemon juice

1 tsp honey

Pinch of salt

BLANCHED GREENS

1 bunch Swiss chard, chopped into 1-inch pieces

Olive oil

SCRUNCHIONS AND COD

7 oz (200 g) scrunchions

4 portions (5 oz/150 g each) fresh cod (not frozen; halibut also works)

Salt and ground black pepper

My mom's partner, Bob, lives in Newfoundland. Every week, he buys fresh cod from his local fishmonger. When he comes to visit, he brings a bag of it in his suitcase, along with a bag of scrunchions (cubed salted pork fat) to cook the cod with. You fry the scrunchions until they go golden and the fat renders out, then drop in the cod and cook it quick, just a couple minutes each side. It always comes out incredible.

At Heart's, we make a brown butter and sherry vinaigrette for our halibut dish, so I took that idea and combined it with Bob's cod and scrunchions. Turned out to be a hit.

MAKE THE VINAIGRETTE: In a small pot over medium heat, melt the butter and cook until it turns a deep golden brown and smells nutty. Remove from the heat and let cool for 10 minutes. Whisk in the sherry vinegar, lemon juice, honey, and salt.

BLANCH THE GREENS: Bring 1 cup of salted water to a boil in a medium pot. Add the chard—stems first, leaves on top—so the stems boil while the leaves steam. Blanch for 3 minutes, then use tongs to stir the leaves into the water to make sure they're cooked through. Cook for another 30 seconds. Drain any remaining water, toss with the olive oil, cover, and set aside.

COOK THE SCRUNCHIONS AND COD: In a large nonstick pan over medium heat, cook the scrunchions until just golden, stirring occasionally, 3 to 5 minutes.

Pat the cod dry with paper towel, then season with salt and pepper. Add the fish to the hot pan with the scrunchions and cook for 4 minutes on one side, until golden and fanned out. Gingerly flip and cook for another 2 minutes, tops.

Divide the greens among the centers of four plates. Top with the cod, golden side up. Drizzle with the vinaigrette and finish with a few scrunchions.

Steak and Dijon Stew *with* Root Vegetables

SERVES 4

- 3 baby-sized turnips, quartered
- 1 parsnip, roughly chopped
- Olive oil
- Salt and ground black pepper
- 1 lb (450 g) 1½-inch-thick top sirloin, cut into 1-inch cubes (ask for one that has some age on it)
- 1 onion, diced
- 2 garlic cloves, smashed
- 1 cup button mushrooms, quartered
- 3 sprigs fresh thyme
- ½ cup red wine
- 1 tsp all-purpose flour
- ½ Tbsp tomato paste
- 2 potatoes (Yukon Golds or Russets), peeled and cut into 1-inch pieces
- 4 cups chicken stock
- 1 Tbsp soy sauce
- 1 tsp pure maple syrup
- ¾ Tbsp Dijon mustard

I'd been working on this stew for a long time. I was trying to get it to taste like a steak pie in stew form, but something was always missing. Then one night, I was on a call while making the stew, just going through the motions, not overthinking, and it worked. A toasted baguette rubbed with olive oil, tomato, and garlic would be damn good with this.

Preheat the oven to 375°F.

Place the turnips and parsnip on a baking sheet. Drizzle with olive oil and season with salt and pepper. Cover with foil and roast until tender, about 30 minutes.

Meanwhile, season the steak cubes generously with salt and pepper. Heat a large, heavy-bottomed pot over medium heat, add a drizzle of olive oil, and sear the beef until it's golden on all sides.

Add the onion, garlic, mushrooms, and thyme to the pot and sauté for 5 minutes. Pour in the red wine and let it reduce for about 2 minutes. Stir in the flour to coat everything, then add the tomato paste. Cook that out for another minute or so.

Now add the roasted veg and the potatoes. Pour in the chicken stock, soy sauce, and maple syrup. Bring to a strong simmer, then cover with a sheet of parchment paper and cook for about 55 minutes, stirring occasionally. You're looking for it to reduce by about a quarter and for the meat to be fork-tender. Right at the end, stir in the mustard. Taste, adjust the seasoning if needed, and serve immediately.

Dara's Roast Duck

SERVES 4

- 1 whole duck (about 3 lb/1.4 kg)
- 2 Tbsp coarse salt
- 2 Tbsp whole black peppercorns
- 1 tsp ground coriander
- 3 carrots, cut into large pieces
- 3 celery stalks, cut into large pieces
- 2 onions, cut into wedges
- ¼ cup all-purpose flour
- 2 cups chicken stock
- 3 Tbsp soy sauce

My friend Dara has a force to her cooking and a sense for appetite, timing, and fearlessness. It's like she embodies the wildflowers and all their medicine that grow around her farmhouse. Some nights at her and Daren's farm—just down the road from Heart's—there are big farm-cut steaks grilled over an outdoor fire with crushed wild juniper, laced with olive oil, black pepper, and salt, and served with a green, herby romesco-esque sauce mortared with garlic and walnuts, or a slaw of grated cabbage, carrot, lemon, and garlic.

But the absolute pinnacle of all Dara's powers is when she roasts a duck. What most cooks find an intimidating endeavor, Dara just gets it done her way, with instinct and an "ah shucks" flair. The duck comes out glistening, tender, and juicy, smelling incredible, as if she has a blueprint inside her for how to cook it. And the next day, she turns the carcass and leftover meat into a pho (page 227) with star anise, chili, coriander, and homemade noodles, and says, "what's the big deal," which only adds to the magic of it all.

PREP THE DUCK: Two to 3 days before roasting, make space in your fridge. Wash and dry the duck thoroughly, then prick the skin all over to help render the fat and crisp the skin as it roasts.

In a spice grinder or using a mortar and pestle, grind together the salt, peppercorns, and coriander. Rub the spice mix all over the duck—inside and out. Place it on a rack set over a large baking sheet so air can circulate underneath. Refrigerate, uncovered, for 2 to 3 days.

Preheat the oven to 350°F.

ROAST THE DUCK: Place the duck upside down on a rack in a large roasting pan. Scatter the carrots, celery, and onions under the rack.

CONTINUES

TABAC HACK

If there's any duck left over, save it for the Duck Pho (page 227). It's the best part of roasting a duck. Make sure to save everything in the roasting pan as well—it all goes into the pho broth.

Roast for 1½ hours. Carefully flip the duck right side up. (This crisps the skin all around. If skipping the flip, start right side up from the beginning.) Continue roasting until the internal temperature reaches 165°F. Increase the oven temperature to 425°F and finish cooking the duck for 20 to 25 minutes, until golden brown.

Remove the duck from the pan and let rest before carving. Save the carrots and celery for stock and set aside.

MAKE THE GRAVY: Remove some of the excess fat from the pan drippings, making sure you've still got a generous amount. Place the pan over medium heat. Add the flour, stirring to make a roux, and brown for a few minutes. Whisk in the stock. Stir in soy sauce for color and season with salt to taste. Simmer for 10 minutes, until thickened. Pour the gravy through a strainer set over a pot.

Carve the duck and serve it with the gravy and the roasted onions alongside.

Duck Pho

SERVES 4 TO 6

Leftover duck skin, carcass, and roasted carrots and celery from Dara's Roast Duck (page 223), divided

1 onion, quartered

2-inch knob ginger, roughly sliced

4 whole star anise

1 tsp black peppercorns

1 lb (450 g) thin rice vermicelli noodles

1 tsp fish sauce

2 tsp soy sauce

Salt, to taste

1 small head bok choy, chopped

Leftover duck meat, shredded (page 223)

5 eggs, beaten

Chili oil or Mexican Chili Crisp (page 286), for serving

TABAC HACK

If your duck is a little lean on meat, you can add a whole chicken or a few raw chicken legs into your broth assembly. Pull the meat out after 1 hour and set aside to cool, so you can shred the meat and add it to your pho. This will give your broth more depth—and meat.

To be in a farmhouse in winter, snow falling in the dark, wind rattling the windows—and to eat homemade pho by candlelight at a table my friend Daren built in the barn at his and Dara's farm—is its own kind of magic. And it was real. Dara's way of putting it together is beautiful, a little chaotic, but full of instinct.

In a large pot over medium heat, combine any leftover duck skin, along with onions, ginger, star anise, and black peppercorns. Let everything brown and release aroma, about 3 to 5 minutes. (If you've already eaten all the skin, you can dry roast the onions, ginger, and spices in the pot instead to deepen the flavor.)

Add the duck carcass, along with the roasted carrot and celery bits if you have them. Pour in enough water to cover everything, about 12 cups. Bring to a boil, then lower to a simmer and cook for a long time, about 1½ hours. Skim off any foam or fat that floats to the top as it cooks.

Strain the broth and return the clear broth to the pot.

Now's a good time to start cooking your noodles in a large pot of salted boiling water. Cook them according to package instructions. Once cooked, strain and rinse with cold water. Set aside.

Season the broth with the fish sauce, soy sauce, and salt to taste. Add the bok choy and the shredded duck meat to the broth. Let it simmer gently until the bok choy softens, about 3 to 5 minutes.

Beat the eggs and slowly drizzle them into the lightly bubbling broth, stirring gently to create thin ribbons.

Place a handful of noodles into each bowl. Ladle the hot soup into the bowls, and drizzle with chili oil.

Crème Brûlée

SERVES 6

2 cups heavy (35%) cream

1 vanilla bean (or double the extract below if not using the bean)

5 egg yolks

7 Tbsp sugar, divided

1 Tbsp pure vanilla extract

This was one of the first desserts I learned how to make. My friend Chris taught me how when I worked at his first restaurant. He'd make it with a shot of Pernod and orange zest. But this is the classic vanilla version we do at Union and Heart's. If you want to swap in pastis for the vanilla extract, go for it. And add some orange zest as well, if you want to nod to the original.

TABAC HACK

If bubbles do form when you're whisking in the cream, light the torch and gently flash over the tops of the filled ramekins to pop the bubbles.

Pour the cream into a saucepan. Split the vanilla bean lengthwise. Use the back of a knife or the edge of a spoon to scrape out the seeds from both halves. Add the seeds to the cream. Set over medium-low heat and let it steep gently for 3 to 5 minutes. Don't let it boil. Set aside and let cool to room temperature. (If it's too hot, it'll scramble the yolks.)

While the cream is cooling, get a large dry stainless steel bowl. Add the egg yolks, 3 Tbsp of the sugar, and vanilla extract. Whisk the hell out of it until the yolks turn a lighter, creamy yellow. You want zero dark yellow streaks, but rather, one smooth, pale mixture.

Preheat the oven to 350°F.

Once cooled, strain the cream, scraping the underside of the strainer. Add the cream to the yolk mixture and whisk gently to combine, creating minimal bubbles (see Tabac Hack).

Set six 4 oz ramekins in a lasagna dish or a half hotel pan—anything deep enough to hold water around the ramekins. Fill the ramekins with the custard mixture (use a pitcher for control), dividing evenly. Carefully pour warm water into the pan until it comes halfway up the sides of the ramekins. Don't go higher. If water spills into the custard when you're moving the pan, it'll wreak havoc with the custard.

Gently transfer the pan to the oven. Bake for 55 to 60 minutes, until the custards are just set, with a slight wobble in the middle. Let cool.

CONTINUES

Chill the cooled custards in the fridge until cold, for 2 to 4 hours.

Right before serving, sprinkle 2 tsp sugar per ramekin in a thin, even layer on top. Wipe the rims of the ramekins to avoid cleaning off burnt sugar later. Hold a brûlée in one hand and a lit kitchen torch in the other. Move the flame slowly over the surface, rotating and tilting the brûlée as you go. The sugar will melt, then caramelize into a glossy, crackling ice rink.

Pouding Chômeur aux Bananes

SERVES 6

A spin on Quebec's "poor man's pudding," this version is a tribute to my grandmother, who liked to flambé bananas on Saturday nights and serve them with ice cream.

BANANA CARAMEL

¼ cup packed brown sugar

4 Tbsp butter

2 bananas, sliced into rounds

1 Tbsp cognac

¼ cup pure maple syrup

½ tsp salt

CAKE

1¼ cups all-purpose flour

½ cup white sugar

2 tsp baking powder

½ tsp salt

1 egg

½ cup milk

3 Tbsp butter, melted and cooled slightly

Whipped cream, for serving

MAKE THE CARAMEL: In a saucepan over medium-high heat, melt the brown sugar and butter, then cook to a light caramel. Add the bananas and cognac, and use a kitchen torch to flambé the cognac. Ensure that you don't break up the banana slices—you want them to keep their shape. Cook for a few more minutes, then add the maple syrup and salt and set aside.

Preheat the oven to 325°F. Grease six 6 oz ramekins.

MAKE THE CAKE: Sift the flour into a large bowl, then add the sugar, baking powder, and salt and mix well.

In a separate bowl, whisk together the egg and milk. Pour the egg mixture into the flour mixture and whisk until smooth and light. Stir in the melted butter until combined.

Divide the caramel amongst the ramekins, making sure each one has five or six banana slices nestled in the caramel at the bottom. Pour the cake batter over the syrup—do not stir.

Bake for about 30 minutes, until the top is golden and a toothpick inserted in the center comes out clean.

Let cool for 10 to 15 minutes before unmolding. Run a thin knife around the edge of each ramekin, invert onto a plate, and lift the ramekin off. Spoon any sauce left in the ramekin over the top. Serve warm with whipped cream.

Chocolate Cake *with* Peanut Butter Mousse

SERVES 8

CHOCOLATE CAKE

1 lb (450 g) butter

1 cup semisweet chocolate chunks or pellets

¾ cup white sugar

¼ cup packed brown sugar

1 tsp pure vanilla extract

Pinch of salt

8 eggs

PEANUT BUTTER MAPLE MOUSSE

2 cups heavy (35%) cream

3 Tbsp peanut butter (smooth or crunchy)

2 tsp pure maple syrup

1 tsp pure vanilla extract

Pinch of salt, if needed

I am always on the hunt for simple desserts to make. This is my friend Daren's go-to chocolate cake at the Galaxy Farm. He made it when we were up for the duck dinner (page 223)—we had it for dessert. As I was eating it, I came up with this peanut butter mousse in my head to go with it. I made it for lunch the next day. It just makes the chocolate cake pop.

Preheat the oven to 375°F. Butter an 8-inch springform pan.

MAKE THE CAKE: In a heatproof bowl, combine the butter and chocolate. Place over simmering water in a double boiler on medium-low heat. Stir until melted and smooth.

Remove from the heat and stir in the white sugar, brown sugar, vanilla, and salt. Let cool slightly (just enough that the eggs won't scramble when you add them).

Fold in the eggs, one at a time, mixing gently until fully incorporated.

Pour the batter into the prepared pan. Bake for 35 minutes, until the center still jiggles slightly but feels set. Let cool completely in the pan, then release.

MAKE THE MOUSSE: In a large bowl, using an electric mixer, whip the cream until it's about three-quarters of the way to soft peaks, about 2 to 3 minutes. Add the peanut butter, maple syrup, and vanilla. Continue whipping for about 15 seconds, then fold with a spatula until smooth and fully incorporated. Taste and, if your peanut butter isn't salted and you find it's needed, adjust with a pinch of salt.

Slice the cooled cake and serve each portion with a generous heap of mousse.

LE TAMBOUR
TAVERN

Le Tambour

Le Tambour

Le Tambour was the name of the first place Chris and I ate when we moved to Paris. We had been out all night drinking demis (half-size beers), standing wide-eyed and laughing together at zinc- and marble-topped bars all over the city. Around three in the morning, we stumbled past a big wood counter. The entrance was tucked off to the side, and a heavyset older Parisian man with big forearms greeted us gruffly (but without judgment) and led us to a table. We went up a couple of steps into a room with a long banquette, shelves full of books, trinkets, and old photos with warm, dim lights hanging above. I remember seeing big ham hocks floating around the room too. The room was smoky, smelled like steak, and was full of chatter and clinking. It was like being awake inside a dream.

We ordered red wine, which came in carafes. Chris had bavette frites, and I had a lamb shank smothered in a piping-hot, rich sauce. We giggled and ate like a couple of kids. It occurred to me that this was how a restaurant should feel: joyful and bold. I loved that it was a refuge from the early-morning cold and the hungry streets. It left an imprint on me—a young man on his first night in Paris.

I was lucky to catch a glimpse of Le Tambour; it was a living time capsule of what taverns and brasseries in Paris used to be. As the euro came into effect, prices went up, and the old restaurant guard gave way to the new. Everything got a little more expensive, and a little more mediocre. Le Tambour is now just a memory of what it was. But the warmth and heartiness of that smoky, dreamlike room stayed with me, and I still chase it. So when an opportunity came to open a place in an old corner tavern with a stoop, I had to go take a look.

It was in Hamilton, Ontario, a city I'd always wanted to live in because it felt like Toronto used to feel when I was growing up in the 90s: a little rough, a little raw, but with an unassuming coolness and creativity. When I first saw the place, it reminded me of taverns in Chicago and Baltimore, both in real life and in movies. The inside was already gutted, exposing brick and steel. It was known in Hamilton as an iconic punk music venue called This Ain't Hollywood.

During my first walkthrough, what caught my eye was the imprint of a fireplace in the back. I imagined a big stone fireplace to cook on. My great-grandfather Ernie built a cabin with a big gray granite fireplace, and on cold, rainy nights late in summer, my grandfather would grill steaks there. He'd marinate them and cook them in the fireplace, and we'd roast marshmallows afterward. I wanted a place to grill steaks—to feel the warmth of a roaring hearth and fill the air with the smells and ambiance of a good French tavern. To have the scent of fire drifting out onto the street, so when you walked by, you couldn't resist stepping inside.

I named it Le Tambour, paying homage to that first night in Paris, when I was most raw and most inspired. I left the old doors covered in punk and rock-and-roll stickers, to honor what the space had been. I hired a couple of Hamilton stonecutters to build the fireplace with stones like the ones Ernie used. When you walk in now, you see the fire in the back and a big horseshoe bar up front. Barbara Klunder painted another mural, and my friend Daren worked his magic with wood and staining concoctions. My friend Josh built the bar and the lights. It all came together in a burst, a kind of crescendo. A kaleidoscope of moments and expressions that became something incredible.

Twenty-five years ago, I walked into a restaurant in Paris. I was still just a kid, but I knew what I'd come for. And today, Le Tambour—*my* Le Tambour—feels closest to that original impression. It's a place that demands presence, creativity, joy, and constant action. There's no room for hand-wringing and second-guessing. It demands that you be fully on board. I try to pass that on to the cooks. I tell them: Keep it simple and don't hold back. Be bold and make the food hot without getting too caught up with plating, because the food loses life in moments of hesitation. But most of all, cook with your heart, with your whole self, with a loving force like those older French cooks at the original Le Tambour.

That's what this place demands. It's a place with live fire and a musical soul, in a hard-working steel town that fosters artists, dreamers, and legacies built from steel, brick, and mortar. Le Tambour has space for it all, including the memories left behind and the ones we carry in. It invites you to eat well, while telling you what it wants to be: loud and joyful. It wants records playing, live music pouring out of big old speakers, steaming-hot ham hocks coated with sauce, and fire-grilled steaks on cutting boards with hefty, crisp French fries and peppercorn sauce. That kind of place. In that kind of town. When I cook at Le Tambour, it feels like I get a real shot to hold space as an artist; I cook completely with my heart, fearlessly, and see where it goes.

I often wonder what my dad would think of all this. He'd be 84, just like Bob Dylan. I can picture him stepping up on that stoop and walking through the big Le Tambour door. He'd glide over to the bar, order a dry martini with an olive, and smile.

LE TAMBOUR
345

French Omelet *with* Feta Dressing

SERVES 2

FETA DRESSING

1.1 lb (500 g) feta cheese

Scant 1 cup sour cream

1 Tbsp chopped fresh oregano

1½ Tbsp lemon juice

1 tsp honey

½ tsp ground black pepper

OMELETS

6 large eggs, divided

2 Tbsp butter, divided

Salt

2 handfuls grated Comté cheese, divided

Ground black pepper

When I was opening Côte de Bœuf, I hired a friend to build the butcher table in the back. I asked him to design the metal bridge-like supports between the big wood legs to echo the style of the Bloor Street Viaduct in Toronto, in homage to the Macedonian ironworkers who built it, swinging on ropes in the darkness, 50 feet down, trying to make a life for themselves.

This omelet conjures up the old diners I imagine these ironworkers might've gone to in the chilly early mornings of another time. I can see those diners—low swivel stools bolted to the floor, packed with bridge builders, their huge arms and hands resting heavily, hunched over counters and wooden shelves, under dim diner lights, with smoky flat-tops full of eggs and peameal. Big frosted picture windows looking out onto the street, streetcars rumbling along.

TABAC HACK

Warm your plates in a 200°F oven. Warm plates at breakfast just make it so much better.

MAKE THE DRESSING: Crumble the feta into a food processor. Add the sour cream, oregano, lemon juice, honey, and pepper. Process until smooth, scraping down the sides as needed. Taste and adjust the seasoning. Set aside.

MAKE THE OMELETS: Crack three eggs into a bowl and whip.

In an 8-inch nonstick pan over medium-low heat, melt 1 Tbsp butter. Just before it starts to sizzle, pour in the eggs. Let them cook for 45 seconds. Using a spatula, gently pull the edges toward the center while tilting the pan so more uncooked egg runs into the gaps. Let that cook, and repeat until there is no wet egg left on top. Season with salt and sprinkle with a handful of grated cheese.

Hold the pan with your left hand (or right, if you're a lefty), angled slightly toward you. Using the spatula in your dominant hand, gently roll the omelet over itself—twice, if necessary—so it looks like a burrito. Let it roll out of the pan onto a warm plate.

Repeat with the remaining ingredients for the second omelet.

Spoon 2 Tbsp of the feta dressing over each omelet, and season again with salt and pepper.

Tambour Buttermilk Wedge Salad *with* Polenta Croutons

SERVES 6

BUTTERMILK DRESSING

1 tsp fennel seeds

1 cup sour cream

1 cup buttermilk

Juice of 1 lemon

1 garlic clove

1 tsp honey

Handful fresh dill

2 sprigs fresh thyme, leaves stemmed

Healthy pinch of salt

Healthy pinch of ground black pepper

POLENTA CROUTONS

Polenta, cooked and chilled as described in Polenta Gratin (see page 117)

1 cup canola oil

WEDGE SALAD

1 head iceberg lettuce

3½ oz (100 g) mild blue cheese

½ bunch fresh chives, chopped

Salt and cracked black pepper

What excites me about Le Tambour is that it feels like it can be anything it wants to be. It's got that French tavern feel, with steaks on the fire, but it also leans into being an old American bar and, with its corner stoop and vibrant, gritty town backdrop. We add this salad to the chalkboard once in a while to bring out that spirit. I like the playfulness of it, the way the golden, hot polenta croutons cut through the cold crispness of the iceberg, the lushness of the blue cheese, and the creamy tang of the buttermilk dressing.

Preheat the oven to 375°F.

TOAST THE FENNEL SEEDS: Place the fennel seeds on a small baking sheet. Toast in the oven for 4 to 5 minutes, until browned and fragrant. Use a spice grinder or a mortar and pestle to grind them.

MAKE THE DRESSING: In a blender, combine the sour cream, buttermilk, lemon juice, garlic, honey, ground fennel, dill, thyme, salt, and pepper. Blend until smooth. Set aside.

MAKE THE CROUTONS: Cut the polenta into 1-inch cubes. In a medium saucepan, heat the canola oil over medium heat to about 370°F. Fry the polenta cubes, turning so all sides go golden brown. Transfer to a plate lined with paper towel to drain.

ASSEMBLE THE SALAD: Cut the iceberg into six wedges. Spoon a generous pool of buttermilk dressing on each plate. Place a wedge of lettuce on top. Spoon more dressing over the wedge. Crumble the blue cheese over top. Scatter the warm polenta croutons on and around the wedge. Finish with chives, a pinch of salt, and cracked black pepper.

Hot Smoked Trout Salad *with* Pernod Dressing

SERVES 4

PERNOD DRESSING

2 egg yolks

Juice of 1 lemon

2 Tbsp Pernod liqueur

1 tsp toasted fennel seeds, ground (a mortar and pestle work)

1 tsp Dijon mustard

¾ cup canola oil

Kosher salt

SALAD

4 Hot Smoked Trout fillets (page 250), broken into pieces

1 big head radicchio, chopped

2 yellow beets, boiled, peeled, and quartered

Squeeze of lemon juice

TABAC HACK

This salad is great with toasted baguette or croutons to add some crunch. To make croutons, cut up a baguette and toss the chunks on a baking sheet with a healthy dose of olive oil, salt, and pepper. Bake at 375°F for 5 minutes, stirring at the 3-minute mark.

We smoke a lot of trout at Le Tambour, like we do at Union, for brunch and lunch. We cure it overnight, then put it into the Big Green Egg the next day with applewood chips and charcoal. You don't need a smoker to make it—any charcoal barbecue will work. The key is the cure, which gives the surface a nice leathery texture. The smoke needs something to cling to, and the result is sweet, salty, and smoky. We use the smoked trout in omelets and fish cakes, but it's also great as an appetizer on toast, with crème fraîche, thinly sliced red onion, a squeeze of lemon, and fresh basil.

MAKE THE DRESSING: In a blender or food processor, combine the egg yolks, lemon juice, Pernod, fennel seeds, and mustard. Blend until smooth. With the motor running, slowly stream in the oil to emulsify. Season with salt to taste. The dressing should be creamy and pourable. If it's too thick, add more lemon juice to loosen it. Place any leftover in a sealed container for up to 1 week.

MAKE THE SALAD: In a large bowl, toss the trout, radicchio, and beets with about 3 Tbsp dressing.

Plate in small bowls, piling the salad in the center and avoiding the rims. Finish with a squeeze of lemon over each salad.

CONTINUES

HOT SMOKED TROUT

MAKES 4 FILLETS

- 5 cups packed golden brown sugar
- 4 cups salt
- 4 steelhead trout fillets (about 21 oz/600 g total)
- 2 handfuls of wood chips (apple or cherry work best)

In a large bowl, mix the sugar and salt together. Lay the trout in a 9 × 13-inch container or pan and spread a handful of the cure evenly over the flesh side of each fillet—don't pack it on. Flip and do the skin side the same way. Cover and let the trout sit overnight in the fridge, turning them over before you go to bed.

An hour before you plan to smoke the trout, submerge the wood chips in water to soak, so they don't burn too fast.

When you're ready to smoke, bank the hot coals on one side of the barbecue and add the wood chips. Place the trout on the grill side opposite the coals, so they're not directly over the heat. Put the lid on, with all the vents open on the bottom and halfway open on top so the fire doesn't choke itself out. Smoke for 3 to 4 hours, checking regularly, until the trout are rosy, sticky, and golden. You may need to add more wood chips about halfway through.

Leftover smoked trout can be stored in an airtight container in the fridge for up to 5 days.

Pan-Fried Pickerel on Toast *with* Harissa Gribiche

SERVES 4

HARISSA GRIBICHE

5 eggs

1 shallot, finely diced

½ cup chopped Bread-and-Butter Pickles (page 280) or dill pickles

2 Tbsp Aioli (page 285) or mayonnaise

1 tsp Dijon mustard

3 Tbsp Homemade Harissa (page 287), plus more to serve

Salt and ground black pepper

PAN-FRIED PICKEREL

1 Tbsp duck fat or olive oil, for toasting

4 slices quality bread

1 cup tempura batter mix (I prefer Nissin brand)

¼ cup soda water

2 ice cubes

4 skin-on pickerel fillets (about 5½ oz/160 g each), each cut into 3 pieces

2 cups canola oil

GALAXY FARM SLAW

½ head green cabbage, grated

2 carrots, peeled and grated

Juice of 1 lemon

1 garlic clove, grated

1 tsp salt

½ bunch fresh cilantro, chopped

4 lemon wedges

I imagine the 1950s, when my grandfather used to fish with his father. Heading up north on a cool, windy spring day with big wool coats on amongst bending jack pines. Trudging through the turpentine-colored maple and oak leaves to their boat. Fishing all morning, then coming back to fry up some pickerel for lunch, fire going.

Pickerel feels like the ocean's gift to the Great Lakes. It's a flavorful white fish with amazing texture. You can get the skin golden and crisp, and it's forgiving (and loving) to cook. Sauce gribiche and pickerel just make sense together. The harissa pulls it into the present.

MAKE THE GRIBICHE: Bring a pot of water to a gentle boil. Gently lower the eggs into the boiling water. Cook for 8 minutes. Leave them in the water and set aside, off the heat, for 5 minutes. Remove the eggs from the water and peel.

Finely chop the eggs and place in a small bowl. Add the shallots, pickles, aioli, and mustard, then stir in the harissa. Mix gently and season with salt and pepper to taste.

PAN FRY THE PICKEREL: Heat a large pan over medium heat. Add the duck fat and, once it's hot, add the bread in a single layer. Fry for 2 to 3 minutes per side, until golden and crisp. Remove from the pan and set aside.

Place the tempura batter mix in a large bowl. Pour in the soda water and whisk until a medium-thick batter forms. Add a few ice cubes (the colder the batter, the lighter the tempura will be) and whisk. We want a slightly thin batter. As the ice cubes melt, you may need to add a little more mix to keep the right consistency, because it will continue to thin out.

Pat the fish dry with paper towel, then dip the fish in the tempura batter.

CONTINUES

Add the canola oil to the pan and heat it over medium heat. Working in batches, place the fish in the oil. Cook for 2 minutes, until golden and crisp, then carefully flip and cook for another 2 minutes. Transfer the fish to a plate and repeat with the remaining fish.

MAKE THE SLAW: Place the cabbage and carrots in a large bowl. In a separate small bowl, whisk together the lemon juice and garlic until the garlic disintegrates into the juice. Pour the dressing over the vegetables and toss to combine. Add the salt and cilantro, then toss again to mix well.

Place a toasted bread slice on each plate and spoon about 1 Tbsp of the gribiche on top. Lay the pickerel on top of the gribiche. Squeeze a lemon wedge over each fillet. Serve with the slaw on the side.

Haddock Cakes *with* Poached Egg and Old Bay Hollandaise

SERVES 6

EVERYDAY SLAW

- 4 cups pickle brine (from Bread-and-Butter Pickles, page 280)
- ¾ cup white vinegar
- ¼ head green cabbage, shredded
- 1 small carrot, shredded
- 2 Tbsp parsley flakes

HADDOCK CAKES

- 1 claw snow crab (see Tabac Hack)
- 2 Yukon Gold or Russet potatoes, peeled and chopped
- 2 lb (900 g) haddock
- 2 Tbsp brine from Pickled Jalapeños (page 282)
- 4 Tbsp mayonnaise or Malt Mayo (page 285)
- 2 eggs, beaten
- 2 cups panko breadcrumbs
- 3 cups canola oil, for frying

My Belgian friend Johan has owned Le Petit Dejeuner in downtown Toronto for more than 20 years. One fever-dream weekend, he and I built a smokehouse at my family farm. No one thought we'd actually do it, but we did. Later that summer, we catered a job up there—smoked a bunch of salmon, and whipped up tons of hollandaise and béarnaise sauce too. He taught me how to make both. It's in his blood. He makes gallons in his sleep, and they never split. At Le Tambour, we came up with this dish for Saturday brunch. The hollandaise comes from that memory: a little browned butter, a little Old Bay, a good squeeze of lemon to finish. The Old Bay gives it that loving East Coast touch.

MAKE THE SLAW: Combine the pickle brine and vinegar in a medium saucepan and bring to a boil. Place the cabbage and carrot in a heatproof bowl and pour the hot brine over top. Stir to combine, then mix in the parsley flakes. Once cooled, cover and refrigerate for at least 2 days before serving.

MAKE THE HADDOCK CAKES: Clean the crab claw. Break it at the joints and slice down the middle on a bias to open it up and remove the meat. For the smaller joints, smash them with the back of a knife to release the meat. Set the crab aside. Reserve the leftover shells.

In a medium pot, boil the potatoes and crab shells in salted water until the potatoes are soft and mashable. Pull out the potatoes and transfer to a large bowl—this will be the base that holds the cakes together. Discard the crab shells at this point too.

CONTINUES

OLD BAY HOLLANDAISE

½ lb (225 g) unsalted butter

2½ tsp white vinegar, divided

5 egg yolks

Juice of ½ lemon

Salt and ground black pepper

1 tsp Old Bay seasoning, plus extra for garnish, if desired

6 eggs

TABAC HACK

We do a version of this at Union with haddock and smoked trout, so if you don't have crab and have leftover smoked trout (page 250), you can use that instead. It gives it a bonito-like flavor.

Add the haddock to the pot of potato water and bring back to a boil, then take it off the heat and let the fish cook gently as the water cools, about 15 minutes. Once cool, strain out the haddock.

Add the haddock and crab meat to the bowl with the potatoes. Add the brine, malt mayo, and a good pinch of salt and pepper. Mix everything together and taste. Adjust with more salt or brine to taste.

Form the mixture into cakes a little smaller than a hockey puck. You want them small enough that they heat through before browning too much.

Set up a shallow bowl with the beaten eggs and a tray with the panko. Dip each cake in the egg wash, then roll it in the panko and set aside. Repeat until they're all coated.

Pour the canola oil into a heavy-bottomed pot and heat it to 375°F. Fry one cake at first to test, then fry one or two at a time once you're comfortable. Cook until golden on both sides and hot through.

MAKE THE HOLLANDAISE: In a small saucepan over medium heat, melt the butter until it foams and just starts to turn golden. You don't want it fully browned, just that light golden nuttiness. That depth adds another layer of flavor to the hollandaise. Once it hits that point, leave it for 30 more seconds, but if it starts to get too brown, pull it off the heat. Set aside.

Fill a medium pot with salted water, add 1 tsp vinegar, and bring to a simmer. This will be your poaching water for the eggs, but before that, you'll use it as a bain-marie for the hollandaise.

Add the egg yolks to a stainless steel bowl that will fit snugly over the pot without touching the water. Add the remaining 1½ tsp vinegar.

Turn the heat off under the pot. Set the bowl over the steaming water, so it doesn't scramble your yolks but instead provides a gentle, forgiving heat. Using a good-quality flexible whisk, beat the yolks with the vinegar until they are a creamy yellow with no visible yolky strands, about 2 to 3 minutes. Check by running the whisk through; the mixture should look smooth all the way through. This part matters. It fortifies the base so when you start whisking in the butter, the sauce is more resistant to splitting.

Start slowly pouring in the butter while whisking. Start with a little at the beginning to temper and not scramble the yolks, then a little more. As you go, you can be more cowboy with it. Pour a little more, then a little more. It will thicken and become mayonnaise-like.

Squeeze in the lemon juice, then season with salt and a touch of pepper. Add the Old Bay and whisk slowly to combine. Remove the bowl from the pot, cover with foil, and set aside.

POACH THE EGGS: Bring the poaching water to a semi-rolling boil. Crack the eggs directly into the water—two at a time, and if you feel confident, go for three. If the eggs sink and sit there, the water's not hot enough. You want them to drop and then roll and dance a bit in the water. That's the sweet spot. If they're vigorously rolling around, the water's too hot. Poach for about 2 to 3 minutes.

TO SERVE: Spoon the slaw onto each plate, set the haddock cakes on top, and finish each with a poached egg. Drizzle the hollandaise over top and sprinkle with more Old Bay seasoning, if desired.

Tambour Tavern Burger

SERVES 4

BURGER SAUCE

2 cups mayonnaise

½ dill pickle, diced

1 Tbsp diced white onion

1 tsp fermented mushrooms (see Tabac Hack), diced

1 tsp Dijon mustard

⅛ tsp Habanero Sauce (page 288)

BURGERS

1½ lb (700 g) ground beef (see Tabac Hack on page 115)

Salt and ground black pepper

4 slices American cheese

4 burger buns

Galangal Glaze (page 287)

Bread-and-Butter Pickles (page 280)

Chopped iceberg lettuce

TABAC HACK

To make fermented mushrooms, pack 7 oz (200 g) chopped cremini mushrooms and ¼ tsp salt into a 2-cup mason jar and seal. Store at room temperature and open the jar every few days to burp it. The mushrooms are ready to use after 2 weeks, and can be stored in the fridge for up to 2 weeks.

It took a while to find out what Le Tambour wanted to be. It used to be a live music venue until the owners had enough and sold it. I kept the band-sticker-covered doors, patched up the tile floor, added a fireplace in the back to cook steaks on, and built a big horseshoe-shaped bar up front. I wanted it to feel accessible, like an everyday stop. A place to grab a beer before catching the train, but also a warm, loving spot for a big steak cooked on a fire. Best way to describe it: a Rochester-style American bar with a French steakhouse feel (with a touch of grunge for good measure). This burger leans into the Rochester side—tavern sauce, American cheese, pickles . . . you get it.

MAKE THE SAUCE: In a medium bowl, combine the mayo, pickle, onion, fermented mushrooms, mustard, and habanero sauce. Stir until combined. Chill until ready to use.

MAKE THE BURGERS: Season the beef with salt and pepper, then shape it into four patties about ½ inch thick.

Heat a heavy-bottomed pan over medium-high heat. Sear the patties for 4 to 5 minutes on one side, until golden and crusted, then flip and place a slice of American cheese on each one. Let the cheese melt while the second side cooks, another 4 minutes, then transfer the patties to a plate and set aside.

Toast the burger buns until just golden.

TO ASSEMBLE: For each burger, spread burger sauce on both sides of a toasted bun, then place the patty on the bottom half. Spoon a little galangal glaze over the burger, add a few pickles, and pile some lettuce on top. Close the burger with the top half of the bun.

Ah Fak, My Daughter Wants Fish for Dinner

SERVES 4

- 3 to 4 lb (1.4 to 1.8 kg) salmon or steelhead trout
- Salt and ground black pepper
- 4 Tbsp olive oil
- 2 Tbsp butter
- 1 bunch fresh tarragon leaves, chopped
- 1 tsp grated ginger
- 1 lemon, halved
- 1 Hungarian yellow pepper, sliced
- 8 to 10 new potatoes

I don't like cooking fish at home. It stresses me out, stinks up the place, and makes me question my worthiness as a cook. But when my daughter became a teenager, she also became a pescatarian—with the exception of spaghetti meatballs, tacos, burgers, and possibly pork tenderloin if we're eating at a friend's house. In a dad frenzy one night, I came up with this recipe. It worked out really well. It's easy, rewarding, and stabilizing.

Preheat the oven to 400°F.

Place the fish skin side down in a roasting dish. Season generously with salt and pepper. Drizzle with the olive oil, letting it pool around the fish.

In a small pan over medium heat, melt the butter. Add the tarragon and stir until the butter is hot and fragrant.

Pour the butter over the fish and sprinkle with the ginger. Squeeze the juice from half of the lemon over top, and scatter a few lemon slices and peppers on the fish.

Roast for about 15 minutes, until the fish is sizzling, opaque, and flakes easily with a fork.

While the fish roasts, add the potatoes to a pot of cold water. Bring to a boil and cook for about 30 minutes, until just tender. Drain, then crush lightly.

To serve, use a spatula to lift a chunk of fish onto each plate. Add the potatoes alongside and spoon some of the buttery tarragon oil over top. Finish with the juice from the remaining lemon half.

Lobster Thermidor

SERVES 4

2 whole live lobsters (1¼ lb/560 g each, or a little bigger) (see Tabac Hack)

Salt, to taste

2 Tbsp butter

¼ small onion, grated

1 Tbsp cognac (or a shot glass of it)

1¼ tsp all-purpose flour

1 cup whole milk

¾ cup grated Comté cheese, divided

4 Tbsp Hotel Butter (page 283)

1 cup panko

1 Tbsp fresh thyme leaves or chopped fresh marjoram

½ lemon

Near the tail end of my time in Paris, living in the 20th arrondissement, I was watching a lot of Hitchcock movies. They'd sell DVDs of them on the street. *Rear Window* was one I'd lean into at night—it would put me to sleep with the rain outside and the comfort of Jimmy Stewart holding watch. There's a scene where Grace Kelly orders lobster thermidor at a fancy New York restaurant. The waiter sets it all up, and there's this shot of the lobsters on a metal tray. That image has always stuck with me. I like the way it shines a light on the 1940s, when restaurants were roaring institutions of luxuriousness and indulgence. I imagine a big steel kitchen. Chefs with tall white hats cleaning hundreds of fresh fat lobsters, juices running everywhere, then baking them off and finishing them under a roaring salamander with cognac, butter, and cheese.

COOK THE LOBSTERS: When I cook lobsters, I start by freezing them for 30 minutes (this puts them to sleep).

Meanwhile, fill a large stockpot with enough water to fully submerge the lobsters. Add a generous amount of salt, so it tastes like seawater. Bring the water to a full, rolling boil.

Remove the rubber bands from the crusher claws, then drop the lobsters head first into the boiling water and boil for 7 minutes. Let them cool.

MAKE THE SAUCE: In a medium saucepan, melt the butter over medium heat. Add the onion and sauté for 1 minute, then hit it with the cognac and let the alcohol burn off for 1 minute. Add the flour and make a wet sand-like roux. Cook, stirring, for another 30 seconds, then turn the burner to low and add the milk, whisking periodically until it thickens. Season with salt, then whisk in ½ cup of the cheese. Remove from the heat and set aside.

CONTINUES

TABAC HACK

When I was in Boston, my cousin's uncle went out and bought 25 lobsters for me to clean and process, and I don't think I ever recovered from that day. You can buy cooked lobster, but they're usually overcooked, and then they're cooked again in this recipe. So I recommend doing the deed yourself. But in a pinch, you can make it work with cooked lobsters.

Preheat the oven to 450°F.

PREP THE MEAT: Remove the two big claws first, then crack them with the back of your knife and remove the meat from the claws and knuckles; give it a rough chop and add it to a large bowl. Cut the lobsters in half lengthwise down the middle, crack them, and take the meat out. Pull the tail meat out as well. Remove the digestive tract and coral, if it's there, and add it to the bowl. Remember to save the tail shells, because the lobster's going back in them. Cut the lobster meat into bite-sized pieces and add it to the bowl. Add the sauce and stir it all together.

Heat a small pan over medium heat. Add the hotel butter, panko, thyme, and 1 tsp salt, and toast until the panko is golden. Toss the panko mixture with the remaining ¼ cup cheese.

Spoon the lobster mixture into the tail shells and set them in a medium baking dish. Sprinkle the panko mixture on top.

Bake in the preheated oven for 5 minutes, then turn on the broiler and broil for 1 minute, until golden and bubbling. Finish with a squeeze of lemon.

Spaghetti and Meatballs

SERVES 4 TO 6

TOMATO SAUCE

- Olive oil
- 1 large onion, diced
- 2 garlic cloves, grated
- 1 tsp (or a good squeeze) tomato paste
- Salt and ground black pepper
- 1 Tbsp Kingsgate Reserve fortified wine (or any fortified wine)
- 1 can (28 oz/796 mL) crushed Roma tomatoes
- 4 cups passata

MEATBALLS

- 1½ lb (700 g) ground beef
- 3 Italian sausages (mild or spicy), removed from casings, or 1½ lb (700 g) ground pork
- 2 Tbsp soy sauce
- 1 Tbsp Dijon mustard
- ½ Tbsp pure maple syrup
- 1 tsp Korean ground red pepper (gochugaru)
- Chili flakes (optional)
- Salt and ground black pepper
- 1 egg (or 1 tsp mayo works)
- ¼ cup milk
- ½ cup breadcrumbs

- 1 lb (450 g) spaghetti
- Piave or Parmesan cheese, for serving

This is my go-to home dinner, which I've been refining over the last 12 years. It's best made in one fluid crescendo of activity. You can freeze half the portion—it's even better the next week. It's a dish that makes both adults and kids happy. Grounding and meditative to make, it's full of love and brings a calmness amidst the weekly chaos of school and phones. It's the kind of meal that says, "Oh yeah, okay, I am still an alright parent."

MAKE THE SAUCE: Set a large, heavy-bottomed pot over medium heat. Add a generous amount of olive oil (three good shots, more than you're used to using). Sauté the onion until soft, then add the garlic, sautéing for another 5 minutes or so. Add the tomato paste and sauté, stirring it in, for 1 minute. Season with salt and pepper, then hit it with a shot of the fortified wine (this will offset the acid in the tomatoes). Let that cook off for a minute.

Add the tomatoes. I use a wooden spoon to crush them a bit. Add the passata. Rinse out both the can and the jar with a splash of cold water, swirl them to get every last bit, and add that too. Give everything a stir, lower the heat, and let the sauce slowly come to a simmer while you make the meatballs.

MAKE THE MEATBALLS: In a large bowl, combine the beef, sausage, soy sauce, mustard, maple syrup, Korean pepper, chili flakes to taste (if using), and a good pinch of salt and black pepper.

In a small bowl, beat the egg with the milk. Add the breadcrumbs and stir until you get a wet, paste-like mixture (not a dry, thick, clumpy one). Add a little more milk if needed. This panade will yield meatballs that are soft and dumpling-like.

CONTINUES

TABAC HACK

I like to have a small bowl close by when I am preparing onions and garlic. As the scraps and skins start accumulating around me, I can just wipe them into the bowl, and it keeps me fluid. It saves me from having to open a cupboard to get to the garbage—and it saves everyone else from having to close the cupboard when I forget.

Add the panade to the meat mixture. Mix everything by hand until fully incorporated. You want it sticky enough to cling to your palm when you turn your hand over. Give it a solid 4 minutes of real squeezing and folding, like you're working dough.

Shape the meat mixture into small balls, about the size of a golf ball. Once they're formed, add the meatballs straight to the sauce, which should be gently simmering by now. Stir them around, partially cover the pot with a lid (or a piece of parchment paper), and cook for 1 hour and 45 minutes, stirring occasionally. For the last 30 minutes, take the lid off so the sauce can reduce.

In a large pot of salted boiling water, cook the spaghetti according to package directions. Drain.

Plate the spaghetti in bowls and scoop the meatballs and sauce over top. Grate a healthy pile of Piave over each bowl.

BOY

Barbecued Habanero Wings

SERVES 4 TO 6

- ¾ cup packed brown sugar
- ½ cup kosher salt
- 4 lb (1.8 kg) chicken wings (flats and drumettes)
- 2 tsp Habanero Sauce (page 288)
- ⅔ cup Rib Sauce (page 131)
- 1 Tbsp Galangal Glaze (page 287)
- 1 Tbsp white vinegar
- 1 Tbsp honey
- 1 Tbsp butter
- 2 dashes Frank's RedHot sauce (optional)

When I was growing up, my friend Tony's Uncle Rick and his dad, Joe, owned a chain of places called Ricki Jo's. Sometimes we'd go to one for dinner before Leafs games, or on weekends before Jays games. We'd catch a ride on their chartered bus to the stadium with a bunch of other regulars. I remember how loud and fun it was on those rides. As we approached the gates, the driver would yell, "Beers down!" and everyone would yell back, "Beers are down!" It felt like the coolest thing in the world to be part of.

Ricki Jo's had the best wings I've ever had. They were kind of sweet, but sour too, with just a bit of heat underneath it all. During the pandemic, when we were doing nothing but takeout, we needed chicken wings. So I leaned into Ricki Jo's wings—and the memories—and came up with these. The wings need to cure for at least 6 hours, so this is a good day-before move. The night before is ideal.

In a large bowl, mix the sugar and salt together thoroughly with your hands. Add the wings and toss them in the cure so they're thoroughly coated. Add the habanero sauce. Mix to combine. Cover and refrigerate, allowing the wings to cure overnight. Or, if you're tight on time, start it in the morning, for dinner that night. As long as they get 6+ hours, you're good.

Rinse the wings under cold water and pat them dry.

Fire up the barbecue to 375°F. If it's charcoal, bank the coals to one side. Add some applewood chips if you want to smoke the wings a bit too. If you're using gas, light one side only. The wings go on the cooler side either way. Grill the wings over the indirect heat for 40 minutes, turning them halfway through.

CONTINUES

TABAC HACK

At Le Tambour, we deep-fry the wings to order and then toss them in sauce, but they're just as good when finished on the barbecue.

Meanwhile, in a small saucepan, combine the rib sauce, galangal glaze, vinegar, and honey. Bring to a simmer over medium heat and reduce, stirring occasionally, for 15 minutes, then add the butter and stir until the sauce starts to look glazy. Sometimes I hack it with a little shot of RedHot for that good, wholesome trashiness.

Place the wings in a large bowl and toss them with half of the sauce. Return the wings to the barbecue, still over indirect heat, for another 20 minutes.

Return the wings to the bowl and toss them in the remaining sauce. They should be puffy, glistening, and very tasty.

BBQ Marinated Bone-In Striploin *with* Smashed Potatoes and Paris Butter

SERVES 2 TO 4

2 to 2½ lb (900 g to 1.1 kg) bone-in striploin steak

BONE-IN STRIP MARINADE

3 Tbsp soy sauce

2 Tbsp Worcestershire sauce

1 garlic clove, smashed and chopped

2 Tbsp ground black pepper

1 Tbsp kosher salt

SMASHED POTATOES

1 lb (450 g) new potatoes, partially peeled (see Tabac Hack)

1 shallot, diced

2 Tbsp olive oil

1 Tbsp butter

Chopped fresh chives (optional)

Salt and ground black pepper

TO SERVE

Paris Butter (page 283), softened

Galangal Glaze (page 287)

Aioli (page 285)

At Le Tambour, we cook big steaks over a fire—I even built a fireplace in the kitchen for it—and do a version of my grandfather Johnny's marinade. He'd load it with finely ground black pepper, a pinch of garlic powder, a pinch of onion powder, a few good shakes of Worcestershire, a couple shakes of soy sauce, and some salt. If he was planning to grill at six p.m., the meat would be marinating by two. These steaks are straight from Sundays at his place in Stouffville.

MARINATE THE STEAK: Lay the steak in a shallow baking pan and pour the soy sauce and Worcestershire sauce over top. Rub the garlic into the meat with your hands, then sprinkle with the pepper and salt. Roll the meat through the mixture until it mops it all up, using the garlic to work it in even more. Use your hands and be rough with it, like you're an old French man who's been in the garden all day. Cover and refrigerate for an hour.

MAKE THE SMASHED POTATOES: Meanwhile, place the potatoes in a pot of salted water and bring to a boil. Boil for about 25 minutes, until soft. Strain, leaving the potatoes and about ½ inch of water in the pot. Add the shallot, olive oil, butter, and chives (if using), then roughly smash the potatoes with a fork. Season with salt and a healthy dose of pepper. It should taste like you're sitting with your grandma at the lake, on the veranda, as the sun sets and dinner's on.

GRILL THE STEAK: Preheat the barbecue. Grill the steak for 10 minutes per side, then let it rest uncovered for 15 minutes, leaving the grill on. Return the steak to the grill for another 3 minutes per side to get it to pop and sizzle again.

CONTINUES

TABAC HACK

Partially peeling the potatoes, zebra-style, doesn't have to take long (they're getting smashed anyway). I just like a little skin off so it doesn't overpower the potato.

TO SERVE: Slice the steak against the grain and arrange the slices on a cutting board or platter. Serve with a scoop of Paris butter on top and some galangal glaze and aioli on the side. Serve the potatoes alongside.

BONUS MARINADE: JOHNNY'S WAY

In a medium bowl, combine ½ tsp onion powder, ½ tsp garlic powder, 1 tsp soy sauce, 1 tsp Worcestershire sauce, 1 tsp black pepper, and ½ tsp salt. In a shallow baking pan, smother the meat in the marinade. Cover and refrigerate for a few hours.

Smashed Potatoes

Maple Croissant Bread Pudding

SERVES 6

5 egg yolks (see Tabac Hack)
½ cup sugar, plus extra for sprinkling
1 Tbsp fresh lemon juice
2 cups heavy (35%) cream
1 cup whole milk
8 croissants, ripped up
3 Tbsp pure maple syrup

TABAC HACK

Use the leftover whites to make the Eton Mess (page 276).

This one was a go-to for my Paris dinners. I always think about economy of movement—this dessert is dead easy, and a huge hit. It'll also buy you time to focus on the other courses.

Place the yolks in a large bowl and add the sugar and lemon juice. Whisk until creamy. Add the cream and milk and whisk until smooth.

Place the croissants in another large bowl (something that'll fit in your fridge). Pour the custard over the croissants—it should just cover them. Cover and refrigerate overnight to soak and allow the flavors to develop.

When ready to bake, preheat the oven to 375°F.

Pour the maple syrup into the croissant mixture and fold it through.

Line a loaf pan (9 × 5-inch) with plastic wrap. Pour in the croissant mixture and fold the plastic wrap over top.

Set up a bain-marie by placing the pan in a larger deep pan and adding hot water around it until it comes halfway up the sides. Bake for 1 hour and 10 minutes, until puffed up and golden. Remove the pan from the bain-marie and let cool.

To serve, slice into 1½-inch slabs—the size of a good banana bread slice. You can warm each slice in the microwave, then sprinkle sugar on both sides and caramelize it in a medium-hot, heavy-bottomed pan. Or sprinkle sugar on one side, sear that side in a hot pan, then flip and finish warming in a 350°F oven.

Eton Mess

SERVES 6 TO 8

BAKED MERINGUE

7 egg whites

½ tsp white vinegar

1½ cups sugar

MACERATED FRUIT

1 pint raspberries

½ pint strawberries, sliced

2 peaches, peeled, pitted, and sliced (see Tabac Hack)

2 Tbsp sugar

1 tsp fresh lemon juice

WHIPPED CREAM

2 cups heavy (35%) cream

1 tsp sugar

1 tsp pure vanilla extract

1 tsp pure maple syrup

Pinch of salt

TABAC HACK

Score the top of the peaches, then blanch in boiling water for 5 seconds. Drop in an ice bath, and the skins will come off right in your hand. (It's just like blanching a tomato.)

This is my go-to dessert during berry season when they are coming in bunches and waves from farmers. The meringue part is the only challenge, but even if they don't come out as well as you like, they still work. Once you have the meringue technique down and in your back pocket, it is just about macerating the berries, whipping some cream, and layering it all together. Always a hit.

Preheat the oven to 200°F. Line a baking sheet with parchment paper.

MAKE THE MERINGUE: In a large bowl, using an electric mixer, beat the egg whites and vinegar until thick and peaky. Slowly start incorporating the sugar, mixing until stiff peaks form.

Scoop the meringue onto the prepared baking sheet in 3-inch peaky round mounds. Bake for 2 to 2½ hours or until a golden hue develops. Turn the oven off and leave the meringues in there.

MACERATE THE FRUIT: While the meringues bake, in a large bowl, combine the raspberries, strawberries, and peaches. Sprinkle with the sugar and lemon juice, toss gently, and set aside.

WHIP THE CREAM: In a large bowl, using the electric mixer with clean beaters, start whipping the cream. Just before it reaches soft peaks, add the sugar, vanilla, maple syrup, and a pinch of salt, then continue whipping for 30 to 45 seconds to combine.

ASSEMBLE THE ETON MESS: Break up the meringues and divide half of the broken pieces among six to eight shallow bowls. Staying toward the center of the bowl and building upward, spoon in some macerated fruit and a heaping spoonful of whipped cream. Add more broken meringue and another spoonful of whipped cream. Finish with more fruit.

Pantry

Bread-and-Butter Pickles

MAKES 6 JARS (ABOUT 1 CUP EACH)

5 lb (2.3 kg) mini cucumbers (or, when in season, gherkin-style work the very best), sliced into ½-inch-thick rounds

2 cups white vinegar

2 cups sugar

⅓ cup kosher salt

1½ tsp yellow mustard seeds

¼ tsp ground turmeric

½ small onion, thinly sliced

TABAC HACK

You can also cowboy up by pickling the cucumbers in a bowl or metal container. Pour the hot brine over the cucumbers, cover with plastic wrap, let cool to room temperature, then refrigerate for up to 1 month. We do this in buckets at Union.

My grandmother made these every summer in July. There'd be jars of them on the counter, and she'd go pick some baby corn from the field next door to pickle too. They were part of the essence of her cooking. They were always on the dinner table, or tucked into sandwiches with leftover steak and mustard the next day.

Sterilize six 1-cup mason jars. Pack the cucumbers into the sterilized jars, dividing evenly.

In a large pot over medium heat, combine the vinegar, sugar, salt, mustard seeds, turmeric, and onion. Stir well to help the sugar dissolve and slowly bring to a simmer, stirring regularly. Don't let it boil; otherwise, it will burn and turn a dark brown.

Ladle the brine over the cucumbers in the jars, making sure they're fully covered. Place the lids and rings on, and tighten gently.

Process the jars in a boiling water bath for 10 minutes (start timing once the water returns to a full boil). Ensure the jars are covered by at least 1 inch of water, then let cool, undisturbed. Check the seals before storing and tighten the lids. Sealed jars can be stored in a cool, dark place for up to 1 year; once opened, refrigerate and use within 3 months.

TOP: Bread-and-Butter Pickles
BOTTOM: Pickled Jalapeños (page 282)

Pickled Jalapeños

MAKES 6 JARS (ABOUT 1 CUP EACH)

- 5 lb (2.3 kg) jalapeños, cut into ½-inch-thick rounds
- 2 cups white vinegar
- 2 cups white sugar
- ⅓ cup kosher salt
- ½ small onion, thinly sliced

TABAC HACK

You can also cowboy it. Pour the hot brine over the jalapeños in a bowl or metal container, cover with plastic wrap, let cool to room temperature, then refrigerate for up to 1 month. We do this in buckets at Union.

When Union first opened, there was a great Cuban-French-style restaurant a few doors down called Deluxe. They did conch fritters with a smoky pepper mayo and pickled jalapeños. My dad and I would sneak in for lunch, or before my shift, and crush a plate of those with a couple of Chardonnays. The pickled jalapeños stuck with me, so I used my grandmother's pickle recipe (page 280), stripped out the turmeric and mustard seeds, and made my own version for Union. They've become part of the essence of Union's food.

Sterilize six 1-cup mason jars. Pack the jalapeños into the sterilized jars, dividing evenly.

In a large pot over medium heat, combine the vinegar, sugar, salt, and onion. Stir well to help the sugar dissolve and slowly bring to a simmer, stirring regularly.

Ladle the brine over the jalapeños in the jars, making sure they're fully covered. Place the lids and rings on, and tighten gently.

Process the jars in a boiling water bath for 10 minutes (start timing once the water returns to a full boil). Ensure the jars are covered by at least 1 inch of water, then let cool, undisturbed. Check the seals before storing and tighten the lids. Sealed jars can be stored in a cool, dark place for up to 1 year; once opened, refrigerate and use within 3 months.

Butters

Variations of these butters are threaded through all the restaurants—they go on steaks and are used to finish sauces. They don't take long to make and they last a while.

HOTEL BUTTER

MAKES ABOUT 2 CUPS

1 lb (450 g) unsalted butter, room temperature and cubed

1 shallot, diced

1 bunch fresh parsley, chopped

1½ oz (3 Tbsp) Pernod liqueur

1 tsp Korean ground red pepper (gochugaru)

Salt and ground black pepper

In a blender, combine the butter, shallot, parsley, Pernod, Korean pepper, and salt and black pepper to taste. Blend until smooth.

Transfer to an airtight container and refrigerate for up to 2 months.

PARIS BUTTER

MAKES ABOUT 2 CUPS

1 lb (450 g) unsalted butter, room temperature and cubed

1 shallot, minced

1 garlic clove, minced

5 anchovies, chopped

2 Tbsp Worcestershire sauce

3 tsp curry powder

2 tsp salt

2 tsp chopped tarragon

1 tsp paprika

1 tsp Korean ground red pepper (gochugaru)

1 tsp Dijon mustard

In a food processor, combine the butter, shallot, garlic, anchovies, Worcestershire, curry powder, salt, tarragon, paprika, Korean pepper, and mustard. Blitz until smooth.

Transfer to an airtight container and refrigerate for up to 2 months.

Chicken, Hen, or Rabbit Brine

MAKES 8 CUPS

- 8 cups water
- 1 Tbsp honey
- 3 garlic cloves, smashed
- 2 bay leaves
- ¾ cup salt
- 1 tsp black peppercorns, smashed a little
- 1 lemon, cut in half
- 1 cup ice cubes

This is the kind of brine we use for anything that needs a little help staying juicy, like chicken or rabbit. It's the same one we use for the Fried Chicken Sandwich (page 119), simple and reliable, doing most of the work before the pan even heats up.

In a large pot, combine the water, honey, garlic, bay leaves, salt, and peppercorns. Squeeze in the lemon juice, then add the halves to the pot. Bring to a boil, remove from the heat, and let it steep for 5 minutes. Add the ice cubes, and let it cool completely.

Add the chicken, hen, or rabbit to the pot, cover, and refrigerate overnight.

Condiments

These are some of the building blocks of Union's flavor that have become components of the recipes in all the other joints. They're sweet, salty, spicy, and bright, the kinds of things that make everything else pop. None of them are complicated, but they're what make the food taste like Union.

AIOLI

MAKES 6 CUPS

- 9 egg yolks
- 1 Tbsp Dijon mustard
- 2 garlic cloves, grated
- 1 tsp white vinegar
- 5 cups canola oil
- ¼ cup mirin (I like Honteri brand)
- 1 tsp salt

In a food processor, combine the yolks, Dijon, garlic, and vinegar. Start blending and slowly drizzle in the canola oil in a steady stream. If you keep the stream consistent, it'll thicken into a tight emulsion.

Thin with mirin to reach the texture you want, then season with salt to taste. Store in an airtight container in the fridge for up to 2 weeks.

VARIATION

Truffle Mayo: Stir 1 Tbsp of Menu brand truffle paste into 1 cup of the aioli.

MALT MAYO

MAKES 6 CUPS

- 9 egg yolks
- 1 Tbsp Dijon mustard
- 5 cups canola oil
- ¼ cup malt vinegar
- 1 tsp mirin (I like Honteri brand)
- 1 tsp salt

In a food processor, combine the yolks and Dijon. Start blending and slowly drizzle in the canola oil until emulsified. Add the malt vinegar, mirin, and salt, blending for a few more seconds to combine. Adjust to taste.

Store in an airtight container in the fridge for up to 2 weeks.

SPICY MAYO

MAKES 6 CUPS

9 egg yolks
1 tsp white vinegar
1 Tbsp sambal oelek (the kind without garlic)
5 cups canola oil
3 Tbsp mirin (I like Honteri brand)
1 tsp salt

In a food processor, combine the yolks, vinegar, and sambal oelek. Blend while slowly streaming in the canola oil until emulsified. Thin with mirin and season with salt. If it's too thick, add a little more mirin.

Store in an airtight container in the fridge for up to 2 weeks.

MEXICAN CHILI CRISP

MAKES ABOUT 2 CUPS

1 (3 oz) bag dried arbol chilis
5 garlic cloves, peeled
1½ cups canola oil
1 tsp kosher salt

Deseed the chiles by breaking them open and gently wiggling them between your fingers so the seeds fall out. Transfer the deseeded chilis to a saucepan with the garlic cloves, lightly crushing the garlic so the cloves lie flat. Add the oil—you want it to just cover the chilis.

Set over low heat and slowly bring to a gentle simmer; slow and low is best so the garlic gradually turns golden as the chilis toast in the oil. Simmer gently for 25 to 30 minutes.

Add the salt, then carefully transfer everything to a blender and blitz until the chilis and garlic are ground into a coarse paste. Scrape and spoon the mixture, along with all of the oil, into a jar. Store in an airtight container in the fridge for up to 6 months.

GALANGAL GLAZE

MAKES 1½ CUPS

½ cup sugar
1 Tbsp water
1 small knob galangal, finely chopped
¾ cup mirin (I like Honteri brand)
½ cup soy sauce (Yummy House brand)

In a medium saucepan over medium heat, combine the sugar and water. Cook until the sugar caramelizes to a light golden color.

Add the chopped galangal and cook briefly, then stir in the mirin and soy sauce. Simmer for 3 minutes, then remove from heat. Store in an airtight container in the fridge for up to 4 weeks.

HOMEMADE HARISSA

MAKES ABOUT 3 CUPS

5 dried poblano peppers
1 handful dried arbol chilis, seeded
3 tsp coriander seeds
2 tsp cumin seeds
1 tsp caraway seeds
3 garlic cloves
2 large red peppers, roasted and peeled
3 Tbsp freshly squeezed lemon juice
2 Tbsp tomato paste
2 tsp smoked paprika
½ tsp sugar
Good pinch of salt
2 Tbsp olive oil

Place the poblanos in a bowl, cover with boiling water, and seal with plastic wrap. Let sit for 30 minutes, until softened. Remove the stems and seeds.

Meanwhile, preheat the oven to 375°F.

Spread the arbol chilis and the coriander, cumin, and caraway seeds on a parchment-lined baking sheet. Toast in the oven for 3 to 5 minutes, until lightly browned and fragrant. Cool before grinding.

Using a spice grinder or a mortar and pestle, grind the toasted chilis and seeds.

In a blender or food processor, combine the ground spices, rehydrated poblanos, garlic, roasted red peppers, lemon juice, tomato paste, paprika, sugar, and salt. Blend until smooth. Add the olive oil and blend until fully incorporated. Taste and adjust the salt as needed. Store in an airtight container in the fridge for up to 2 weeks.

CHILI JAM

MAKES 2½ CUPS

- 1¼ cups sugar
- 1 shallot, thinly sliced
- 1 garlic clove, thinly sliced
- 2½ cups strained sambal oelek
- 3 cups mirin (I like Honteri brand)

In a medium heavy-bottomed saucepan over medium heat, combine the sugar with 1 tsp water. Cook until it turns a dark caramel color.

Add the shallot and garlic and cook briefly until softened. Stir in the sambal oelek until it all comes together, then pour in the mirin. Reduce by half, stirring occasionally, until thick and glossy. Store in an airtight container in the fridge for up to 1 month.

TABAC HACK

Once strained, the sambal liquid can be added to the buttermilk marinade for the fried chicken sandwich (page 119).

HABANERO SAUCE

MAKES 4 CUPS

- 1 lb (450 g) habaneros, seeds removed
- 6 garlic cloves
- 1 tsp kosher salt
- ⅓ cup white vinegar or rice vinegar
- ⅓ cup lemon juice

In a food processor, combine the habaneros, garlic, and salt. With the motor running, slowly pour in the vinegar and lemon juice—about 3 seconds of steady stream—until blended and smooth.

Transfer to a container and adjust with more vinegar or salt to taste. Store in an airtight container in the fridge for up to 1 month.

1. Spicy Mayo (page 286) 2. Aioli (page 285) 3. Chili Jam 4. Bread-and-Butter Pickles (page 280) 5. Pickled Jalapeños (page 282) 6. Mexican Chili Crisp (page 286) 7. Galangal Glaze (page 287) 8. Habanero Sauce

Acknowledgments

Thank you to everyone who has helped me along the way.

My dad for backing Union and giving the place its name.

My mom Jocelyn for your support and love.

My sister Amy for your graphic designs and support.

My brother Chase for having the vision for Côte de Bœuf.

My daughter June.

My grandparents Johnny and June.

Jack Gillies and my Grandmama.

Uncle Bill for your belief in me.

All my cousins, aunts Shelley, Nancy, and Sandy, and uncles Tony, Scott, and Dan.

Both Barbies and my aunt Janet.

Elise for selecting the most legendary baseball walk-up song for me.

Daniel for your genius and awesome food shots.

Rachel for your kind spirit and ability to keep my voice in this book.

Nadia for helping me find my voice.

Julie for always rooting for me.

Jenn for your Bruce Lee wisdom.

Daren and Dara for showing me what magic looks like.

The Sheridans for showing me what the good life looks like.

Danny for your aerospace and cooking all the recipes.

Coco for cutting my hair for the last 35 years and giving me Bowen.

Ralph and Sara for showing me unconditional love.

Robert and Kristin for giving me this opportunity.

Eamon for taking a chance on me and giving me my first job in Paris.

Cindy Mia and Liam for being there for June.

Chris for teaching me how to cook.

Nico for taking a chance on me and letting me cook at your hotel.

Pierre for putting me up in your apartment so I could cook my dinners in Paris.

Tyler for finding Heart's and pushing me to do it together.

Steven for running Union for 14 years and helping me make it into a place full of love.

Damien for putting the French-French into Côte de Bœuf with your food.

Hamish for your great knowledge and loving force in your cooking.

Ross for your awesome force at Union and Heart's.

Shawn for helping me make this happen.

Luke for your stalwart belief in me and Union and managing it through a tough time.

Annie and Andrew for making Heart's so warm.

Britt Fady Nestor for making Tambour an amazing place.

Everyone who has worked at Union, Côte, Heart's, and Le Tambour.

Frank for lugging sides of beef to me every Saturday morning.

Peter for always answering your phone and fixing the stoves and handling various other emergencies.

Charlie for always answering the phone and fixing the fridges.

Richard and Ryan for always being there and fixing every little annoying thing big and small.

The Burlington boys who kept Union's work force going in lean times.

Michael Stadtlander and Fraser Prince for providing a model for what great chefs look like.

Every regular who has given their unwavering support to the restaurants and helped make them become warm vibrant refuges.

And every restaurateur who chose to be bold despite the odds.

Index

D

ERITIF ANISE 00 5 00
AT DU JOUR: 15 00
NDWICH: 6 00 7 00
AJORATION
DE 0 50 DES 22H 00
PRIX SERVICE COMPRIS
J'aime Paris
xposition de Photographies de
Peter Turnley